cookie sensations

creative designs for every occasion

meaghan mountford

Rutledge Hill Press®
Nashville, Tennessee
A Division of Thomas Nelson Publishers
www.thomasnelson.com

Published by Rutledge Hill Press, a Division of Thomas Nelson, Inc., P.O. Box 141000, Nashville, Tennessee 37214.

Rutledge Hill Press books may be purchased in bulk for educational, business, fundraising, or sales promotional use. For information, please e-mail SpecialMarkets@ThomasNelson.com.

Bundles of Cookies® is a registered trademark.

Photographs by Jason Keefer of Beta Photography

Library of Congress Cataloging-in-Publication Data

Mountford, Meaghan, 1972–
  Cookie sensations : creative designs for every occasion / Meaghan Mountford.
      p. cm.
  Includes bibliographical references.
  ISBN-13: 978-1-4016-0288-8 (trade paper)
  ISBN-10: 1-4016-0288-6 (trade paper)
  1. Cookies. I. Title.
  TX772.M68 2006
  641.8'654—dc22
                              2006021521

Printed in the United States of America

06 07 08 09 10 — 5 4 3 2 1

for my mom

contents

Acknowledgments

The first of many to thank are Sarah Kerchner, owner of Bundles of Cookies, and Eric Kerchner for their continued support throughout the writing of this book and the decade preceding. Alas, so much has evolved since that fateful day I picked up my first bag of frosting.

And thanks to Bundles of Cookies would not be complete without recognizing the talented, creative, smart, and ever-hilarious staff (with special praise to those from the early days, Hope Bennett, Kate Belber, and Sophie Larroque).

My husband Greg's prodding and support proved a continual necessity. Also vital were the encouragement and taste testing of my family (Mom, Dad, Bill, Kristen, Elle, Catherine, Scott, and Allison, as well as my extended family and the Marchand side, who never seem to tire of eating my cookies at parties).

I'm surrounded by helpful, ego-boosting friends such as Fresia, Meg, Betty Ann, and many from Georgetown, the cookie store, and Greg's side. And this book would not exist without my literary friends and mentors from American University.

Much is owed to the photographic talents of Jason Keefer for adopting my excitement of cookie beauty and for making my cookies at home on the page.

A thank-you for the bar backdrop goes to the Old Ebbitt Grill in Washington, D.C. Thank-yous for the historical pictures are owed to the Houghton Library at Harvard, Lindy Russell-Heymann and Helen French for the springerle mold, and Connie Meisinger of House on the Hill for the springerle replica.

And nothing would have gotten beyond my computer without my agent, Andrea Somberg, as well as the good people at Rutledge Hill Press, particularly Pamela Clements and Jennifer Brett Greenstein.

Lastly, thanks go to all the cookie eaters and their creative suggestions that have kept Bundles of Cookies thriving and my skills necessarily sharpened for so many years.

Introduction:
An Edible World of Possiblility

The cookie world reaches far beyond dunking a cookie into milk or putting sprinkles on Christmas trees. Dunking and sprinkling are skills most people have, but how can you tell stories, crack jokes, or express your deepest love through a cookie? Well, through the art of cookie decorating, you can do all this and more. You can prepare powder-blue tux cookies for your brother's wedding or give your dad a bright-orange tie cookie for Father's Day. You can give your gardener mom a bouquet of cookie flowers. You can even recreate your stylish friend's favorite purse, dress, and shoes in cookies.

After almost a decade of decorating cookies for a living, I still find the art fun and exciting. For this book, I experimented with recipes and procedures from start to finish outside the cozy land of the professional kitchen. I shunned the infinite supply of wholesale merchandise and the spacious workspace where everything is within a hand's reach. All tools and materials used here are available in craft stores, supermarkets, specialty stores, or on the Internet. To reflect the experience of the home baker, I made hundreds of cookies using the one foot of counter space and the finicky oven my tiny row-house kitchen offers. This book is meant to demystify this fascinating art so any reader can enjoy decorating amazing and

clever cookies. The detailed instructions should cover every question you might have.

Looking at the pictures, you might feel over-whelmed. I've been there myself. I can't guarantee you'll pick up a frosting bag and right away be able to create the Eiffel Tower, Noah's Ark, a pool table, or a Pekingese dog on a cookie (all cookies I have done for customers). But the secret to good cookie decorating is reduced to a simple technique: Outline the design and fill it in. That's it. I'll show you the best ways to prac-tice, great designs to start, and how to fix—gulp!—mistakes, because, let's face it, even the most fabulous and perfect of us make mistakes on occasion.

The cookie world is forgiving. Once you make a frosting design on a cookie, you can always scrape it off and try again, though this means you may go through quite a bit of frosting and consume a few more calories than you intend (if you eat your mistakes). Even without being Picasso (though I often boast that I've put a Picasso on a cookie, as well as a Munch, Van Gogh, and Monet), it is absolutely possible for you to translate a bare cookie into a beautiful, edible concoction with-out using unappetizing, fluorescent, store-bought tubes of toxic-tasting frosting. And you can do this with your own two hands.

Possibilities

Once you learn the basics, the possibilities are limited only to your imagina-tion. Washing machines and laundry baskets, hammers and screwdrivers, gin and tonics, cosmopolitans and martinis, a cat playing a fiddle, the dish running away with the spoon, cars and vans and trucks and buses and trains (almost anything that moves), brains, eyes, lungs, teeth, mac 'n' cheese, peanut butter, burgers and fries, eggs, eggplants, turnips and peas and tomatoes, heels and strappy sandals, prom dresses and bridesmaid dresses, skiers, runners, bikers, soccer players, foot-ball players, cheerleaders, space aliens and UFOs, babies and brothers and sisters and moms and dads, zebras, pandas, bears, frogs, turtles, alligators, moose, den-tal floss, canoes, beach umbrellas, the kitchen sink . . . I could easily fill the pages of this book with all the requests that I've had—both common and bizarre.

And once you learn, you can never go back. You'll envision possibilities for every occasion, holiday, ritual, gift, and special moment. You'll walk in a store and mock the decorated cookies you see and think, "Ha! I can do much better than *that*." And you can.

What's in Store

We'll start with the story of the decorated cookie. Chock-full of historical significance, the decorated cookie has served as a means of conversation and celebration for centuries. Odds are, you will be using your cookies for much of the same. We'll move on to a simple step-by-step guide that covers the basics of cookie decorating. This will help you write your shopping list. Everything you will need is spelled out, and resources are included to help you find supplies, cookie cutters, and frosting colors. I've added a list of definitions in Chapter 2, in case you come across any unfamiliar terms in the book.

Recipes for cookie dough and frosting help build the essentials of the decorated cookie. While you can pretty much use any rolled cookie dough, pay particular attention to the section on frosting. Without frosting of the right texture and consistency, decorating cookies will be much more difficult.

You will find advice and guidance on how to mix colors with frosting dye as well as which colors look best together. You will learn how to assemble a frosting bag and how to use your decorating tips. All of these preparations are vital before we begin to decorate cookies.

We will take the process step by step. While reading other books on cookie decorating, I wondered how readers who have never picked up a bag of frosting would *really* know what they are being asked to do. To simply say "Now, pipe the outline of frosting" hardly seems sufficient. What is "piping" anyway? If you already know the answer, I'll take your piping skills to the next level. If not, you'll learn here. Templates are provided for practicing, and I heartily encourage you to use them.

The design ideas are meant to guide you in your cookie endeavors. Just a sampling of what you will find: spaceship, octopus, pig, football, baby footprint, cocktail dress, butterfly, martini, wedding cake, and lots of holiday cookies. For every design provided, I could have added a dozen more. I hope the wealth of possibilities inspires you to move beyond these ideas to create more of your own. Think big! *Anything* can be drawn on a cookie.

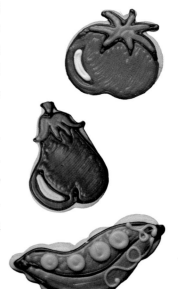

Last, I will offer advice on what to do when you put down the bag of frosting: suggestions on how to make your cookies into gifts and how to clean and store your supplies.

Some Wise Words Before You Begin

Decorating cookies requires many steps and many messy ingredients. It helps immensely to keep your workspace as clean and organized as possible. Often I'll prepare the frosting and all of the frosting bags a day or two before the cookies, or at least earlier in the day. Dividing the tasks makes a long process much more manageable.

Always read through everything first to get the lay of the land. Be mindful of the recipe yields. The yields will help you determine how much you need to purchase and prepare so you aren't missing vital ingredients hours before your party begins.

That being said, don't wait hours before your party begins to start making cookies! We often have customers with last-minute requests such as, "I would like thirty-four gymnasts in yoga poses wearing leopard-print leotards. Can I come back in an hour or should I just wait?" Without a magic wand, an hour is not enough time. We need to make dough, chill it, roll it, cut it, bake it, mix frosting, outline the design, let it set, fill it in, dry the cookies overnight, and wrap them. So if you envision making all the cookie fire truck favors for your son's birthday party, plan on spending a nice long afternoon in the kitchen and some wrapping time the next day. I definitely recommend practicing the technique on an earlier occasion without the pressure to present. Don't decorate cookies for the first time right before a party of expectant, highly judgmental guests.

And now that the lecture is out of the way, enjoy the wonderful world of cookie decorating!

The Story of the Decorated Cookie: Pagan Ritual, Hansel and Gretel, and Beyond

You are creating more than just a mixture of flour, butter, sugar, and dye. The decorated cookie has a rich history steeped in cultural significance and has been a way to convey messages for centuries. The art of shaping dough stretches back thousands of years. Ceramic molds have been found in Egypt and Mesopotamia (now Iraq) from as far back as 2000 BC. In ancient Rome, cakes in the shapes of animals and people were presented to senators as gifts.

Cakes and pastries were popular in seventh-century (AD) Persia (now Iran), one of the first countries to cultivate sugar. With the Muslim invasion of Spain, the Crusades, and the growing spice trade, baked confections soon spread into Europe. It is believed the cookie was invented when bakers used drops of cake batter to test the oven temperature.

By the sixteenth century, the sugar cookie as we know it today was already immortalized in print. A recipe for "fine cakes" can be found in *The Good Huswifes Jewell*, an Elizabethan cookbook by Thomas Dawson, printed in 1596. The recipe calls for "fine flour and Damaske water . . . sweet butter, two or three yolks of eggs and a good quantity of sugar, and a few cloves, and mace, as your cook's mouth shall serve him, and a little saffron, and a little cods [yeast] good, about a spoonful."

1

(and younger sister to the poet William Wordsworth) found gingerbread tasty enough to mention in her journal. In January 1803, despite the bitter cold, she and her brother left home in search of gingerbread to satisfy their cravings.

Gingerbread is not always held in such high esteem in the literary imagination. The British poet, William Cowper, in his 1783 poem *Table Talk* warns of the dangers of falling below one's potential and of settling for lesser substitution: "As if the Poet, purposing to wed, should carve himself a wife in ginger-bread." This notion seems quite a reversal in sentiment from the aforementioned women at fairs eating gingerbread "husbands."

"Hansel and Gretel," from *Hansel and Gretel and Other Stories*, by the Brothers Grimm, illustrated by Kay Nielsen (London: Hodder and Stoughton, 1925).

Typ 905.25.4365 F, Department of Printing and Graphic Arts, Houghton Library, Harvard College Library

Similar to gingerbread, *lebkuchen* was used in Germany to build *Hexenhaeusle*, or "witches' houses," romanticized and popularized by the story of *Hansel and Gretel* when published in 1812 as part of the Grimm brothers' collected German folktales. Hansel and Gretel, seen as a drain on scarce resources, are abandoned by their poor parents despite their father's reluctance. Alone in the woods, their furtive bread crumb trail home eaten by birds, Hansel and Gretel wander for days, starving, until they come across a house "made of bread" with a roof "made of cake and the windows of sparkling sugar." They tear off pieces and stuff themselves, not knowing that the cruel old woman within purposely constructed the house to entice, trap, bake, and eat children. But Hansel and Gretel outfox the old crone and push her into the oven, saving themselves.

Cookies in America

Gingerbread was brought to America by European settlers and was popular at fairs and festivals. New England recipes for flat cookies cut into patriotic shapes were created for the celebrations known as Muster Day and Election Day. Before the Revolution, shapes often depicted a king, but later, the American eagle became a favorite. The cookies were handed out to wives and children when militias gathered for officer election or for military training.

Other cookies had already made their home in America in recipe, if not in name. Martha Washington had in her possession from 1749 to 1799 a handwritten manuscript called the *Booke of Cookery and Booke of Sweetmeats*. This family collection included recipes for "cakes" that are similar to what we today call cookies. For sugar cakes, the baker is instructed to "take 2 pounds of flower, & one pound of sugar, & youlks of 2 eggs, & a spoonfull of sack, & a spoonfull of rosewater, & make it up into paste with melted butter & roule it out pritty thin." A beer glass is suggested to cut the cookies before baking in an oven "meanly hot with stone downe."

In addition to cutting cakes with glasses to shape them, the baker following Washington's cookbook pressed dough into printed molds, as in the recipe for gingerbread. To make this gingerbread, the baker combined boiled honey and vinegar to remove the "scum," and then added strong ale, ginger, licorice, anise seeds, and a "peck of grated bread." Long before the advent of frosting dye in convenient bottles, Washington's cookbook suggested adding claret wine to make "culler'd" (colored) gingerbread.

Cover of Amelia Simmons's *American Cookery.*

Such collections of handwritten recipes were common at this time, as printed cookbooks were scarce. American colonists relied primarily on British presses. Books such as Gervase Markham's early seventeenth-century volume, the *English Huswife*, included advice on cooking, planting, brewing, making clothing, and curing the plague. Its success spurred other publications into the eighteenth century, but British authors paid little attention to the needs of the New World and to American cuisine.

Amelia Simmons's first edition of *American Cookery* in 1796, a practical, inexpensive, paper-covered book, changed this. Her book included recipes such as "Johny Cake" and "Indian Slapjacks" that required distinctly American ingredients. Simmons's is the first cookbook to use the American term "cookie," derived from the Dutch *koekje*.

Noteworthy is the addition of a new cooking method of using chemical leavening in dough, similar to our baking powder or soda. Previously bakers had beat air into eggs, but by 1796, an anonymous American woman had added a chemical to produce carbon dioxide. Simmons's cookbook is the first known to suggest adding pearlash, a substance primarily composed of

AMERICAN COOKERY,

OR THE ART OF DRESSING

VIANDS, FISH, POULTRY and VEGETABLES,

AND THE BEST MODES OF MAKING

PASTES, PUFFS, PIES, TARTS, PUDDINGS,
CUSTARDS AND PRESERVES,

AND ALL KINDS OF

C A K E S,

FROM THE IMPERIAL PLUMB TO PLAIN CAKE.

ADAPTED TO THIS COUNTRY,

AND ALL GRADES OF LIFE.

By Amelia Simmons,

AN AMERICAN ORPHAN.

PUBLISHED ACCORDING TO ACT OF CONGRESS.

HARTFORD

PRINTED BY HUDSON & GOODWIN.

FOR THE AUTHOR.

1796

potassium carbonate and used to make soap and glass, to gingerbread and cookie dough.

Simmons's gingerbread cookie recipe calls for molasses in lieu of treacle to customize the sweet to her American audience. The dough combines cinnamon, coriander or allspice, "four tea spoons pearl ash, dissolved in half pint water," flour, molasses, and butter (she specified "if in summer rub in the butter, if in winter, warm the butter"). The mixture is kneaded and washed with egg whites and sugar.

Simmons's sugar cookie recipe, made with sugar boiled in water, cooled, and combined with pearlash dissolved in milk, flour, butter, powdered sugar, and coriander, is shaped as we do today: rolled half an inch thick and "cut to the shape you please."

Cookie Cutters

In America, wooden molds gradually disappeared in favor of cutters that emphasized the outline of the desired shape. German settlers in Pennsylvania shaped gingerbread by hand into men, often displaying the cookies in windows. The English cut dough with a glass or teacup. Martha Washington's cookbook suggested cutting dough with a beer glass. The idea of placing a metal rim around the outline of a carved mold originated in the mid 1600s, and by 1750 the cookie cutter as a shape independent of a mold came into being.

The nineteenth-century tin industry developed the art of cookie cutters. Tinsmiths had traveling shops, transporting their materials and belongings on wagons. Most carried cutter patterns to ensure uniformity, but they would make cookie cutters to housewives' requests if need be. With increased machinery, by the end of the century cookie cutters were sold in catalogs and stores.

Cookie cutters in shapes such as stars, moons, suns, toys, animals, and humans were hung as tree ornaments. With the rise of Christmas as a commercial holiday, shapes such as wreaths, Santa, and stockings, soon prevailed. American cookie cutters of the 1800s were thick and heavy, usually with flat backs and sometimes with strap handles. Air holes cut in the back allowed air to escape to free the dough from the cutter more easily and were often large enough for a lady's finger to fit through if an extra push was necessary. Shapes at this time included hearts, horses, rabbits, birds, ladies in long dresses, men in high hats, horsemen, leaves, and flowers.

Bridge card party sets, with diamonds, clubs, spades, and hearts, were popular in the early 1900s, available in catalogs such as Sears Roebuck or the Bruce & West Manufacturing Company. With the rise of advertising, baking powder companies and flour mills began to sell cookie cutters with their printed slogans. By the 1920s, cookie cutters were mass-produced in aluminum. Although more choices were introduced, a surprising consistency and uniformity among shapes survived the century, and the basic shapes remain the same today.

But throughout the decades, companies produced cookie cutters unique to their era. Like any relics from popular culture, cookie cutters offer insights into the interests and lives of a generation. Pillsbury released the Comicooky Cutters series in 1937, including paper stickers to apply to the cookies in the likeness of characters from the comic strips *Moon Mullins, Gasoline Alley,* or *Dick Tracy*. In the late 1940s, the Educational Products Company sold Blondie and Dagwood cookie cutter sets, complete with their children, Alexander and Cookie, and Daisy the dog.

Wrigley Spearmint Gum advertised Troll kits for kids through the cookie cutter company Mirro in the mid-1960s. For fifty cents, the kit included an aluminum troll cookie cutter with decorating tips. The instructions recommended sticking on "tiny candies for cooky eyes" or sprinkling the top with "wigs of shaggy, tinted coconut."

Late nineteenth-century cookie cutters.

Plastic cookie cutters became popular in the 1950s. Hallmark introduced its first set of cookie cutters in 1971, offering an incredible variety of brightly colored plastic cutters. Cutter shapes included not only a wide assortment of holiday designs, but also babies, Disney characters, Snoopy and Charlie Brown, the Muppets, and Raggedy Ann and Andy.

Today, you can find copper, aluminum, plastic, or tin cookie cutters in just about any shape you can imagine for the twenty-first century: martinis, the little black dress, an electric guitar, a bikini, a hula girl, a fighter jet, pi, a laptop computer, the space shuttle, and more.

A long history of shaping and decorating cookies precedes us. I'm not sure why these representations seem so specific to sugary treats. I've not heard of a carrot decorated as a British king or a meatloaf made to mimic Raggedy Ann. Perhaps it's the natural indulgence of sweets. There is something powerful and gluttonous about ingesting cookie symbols of religion, popular culture, nature, animals, and characters. We can consume tasty versions of the world by creating edible art—all we need to do is thoughtfully shape the dough and add color.

Bridge card party set of cookie cutters from the early twentieth century.

2

The Shopping Cart:
Everything You'll Need,
Plus Some Baking Terms

Before you walk into a store or browse the Internet to behold the vast world of cookie decorating supplies, it's best to familiarize yourself with the essentials. Cookie decorating is divided into three tasks: making and baking your cookies, mixing and coloring your frosting, and decorating your cookies with frosting. All three tasks can be accomplished from start to finish with ten steps. The instructions in the following chapters will elaborate on these ten basic steps.

Cookies
Step 1 *Make and chill your cookie dough* using your favorite recipe or any of the recipes in this book.
Step 2 *Roll out, cut with your cookie cutters, and bake* the shapes you desire.

Frosting
Step 3 *Mix your frosting* according to the recipes in this book.
Step 4 *Divide your frosting* into separate bowls for as many colors as you will need.

Step 5   *Make your colors* by thoroughly stirring your frosting dye—we will be using a gel paste—into each bowl until you get the desired colors.

Step 6   *Assemble the frosting bag* using the disposable bag, the coupler, and the size tip suggested. (Don't worry, you will learn what these are in this chapter).

Step 7   *Fill your frosting bag* with the colored frosting and tie closed with a rubber band.

Decorating

Step 8   *Draw the basic design on your cookie*, using the provided templates as a guideline, by squeezing frosting ("piping") from your frosting bag using the suggested tip size and color (most often a black frosting or a dark color). Let the frosting set for about ten minutes. This will be your outline.

Step 9   *Fill in the outlined design* using the suggested colors and tips with a back and forth motion from top to bottom, creating lines of frosting to cover the empty space. Squeeze frosting into every nook and cranny of cookie space, but be careful not to cover your outline!

Step 10   *Add details* with frosting using the suggested colors and tips on top of the decorated cookie once the frosting has set.

It will take practice to create smooth lines and a nice, filled-in space without gaps and holes. Many factors affect the finished product, especially your frosting consistency (if your frosting is too stiff, you'll see all of your fill-in lines, but if it's too runny, it may run right off the cookie). But don't be nervous. This book will offer you many opportunities to practice. Luckily, even with little imperfections, these cookies look and taste great. And also keep in mind that these ten steps, even after tons of practice, take a while to complete. I often make the frosting and the frosting bags a few days before I prepare, bake, and decorate the cookies, just to break things up a bit.

The materials you'll need to create your cookies fall into two categories: those that are absolutely necessary and those that are optional, yet recommended. You'll need to have these items on hand before you get started.

Absolutely, Positively Necessary

The following items should top your shopping list. Decorating cookies will go much more smoothly if you have all of these things.

Cookie dough. Any recipe for a good rolled cookie will do, but you'll find recipes for some of my favorites—Sugar Cookies, Almond Cookies, Chocolate Cookies, and Gingerbread Cookies—in Chapter 3.

Cookie cutters. A sharp knife and a template work as well, but a cookie cutter is preferred. Most cookie cutters are either small, about two to four inches, or large, about four to six inches. Either work with the designs in this book and I use both, but intricate designs are more difficult to put on smaller cookies. (See the end of this chapter for great cookie cutter suppliers.)

Rolling pin. You may want to use a cloth rolling pin sleeve to eliminate sticking, particularly if using chocolate or gingerbread dough. A lightly floured rolling pin works just as well, but the flour shows up much more on these darker cookies.

Baking trays. Cookie sheets come in aluminum or stainless steel, though nonstick is the most practical. Insulated trays are good choices, but any thick, solid tray will work. To save time, you should have at least two trays. Cookie dough placed on hot trays spreads, so having extras trays allows you to cool a tray while another bakes.

Standing mixer or electric hand mixer. I use a standing mixer with a flat beater for cookie dough and a wire whip for frosting, but an electric hand mixer also works well to mix your dough and frosting. A mixer, as opposed to your own strong arm, is especially useful for whipping your frosting.

Frosting in the buff. I call frosting without color simply "in the buff." You'll find recipes for both Royal Icing and Buttercream Frosting in Chapter 3. Because the addition of ingredients such as butter or vanilla extract gives freshly mixed frosting a tint of yellow or brown, to make any color, dye *must* be added. This includes white!

Twelve-inch plastic, disposable decorating bags. Also known as frosting bags, these are available at most craft stores and certainly cake decorating supply stores. Bags do come in thick, permanent materials, but I much prefer the disposable ones. The clear bags are perfect for using lots of different colors of frosting. They are inexpensive, so you don't cringe when they rip or have to be thrown away.

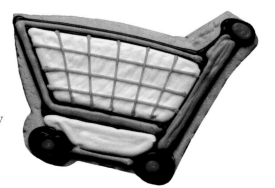

Couplers. Also available at craft and specialty stores, these plastic two-piece thingamajigs consist of a cylinder and a ring; they are usually white or clear. Couplers are used with the decorating bags to hold your tips so you can use any size tip on a bag of frosting. Ideally, have enough couplers so you can make all the frosting bags you need without having to move the coupler from one bag to another.

Tips. Cone-shaped, metal tips fit on the end of couplers over the disposable decorating bags. The openings at the small end of the tips come in all sorts of shapes and sizes to control the frosting as it is squeezed from the frosting bag. For cookie decorating, you only need simple, round tips numbered 1 (the smallest) through 6 (the largest we will use). None of the fancy-schmancy, funky-shaped tips are necessary for these projects. Tips can be found in most craft or cake decorating stores or on the Internet. It is useful to buy several of each tip size, particularly numbers 2, 3, 4, and 5 (see Chapter 5), so you can switch tips without having to take them off another bag and wash them.

Concentrated paste or soft gel paste for frosting color. Frosting color, also known here as dye, comes in both liquids and pastes, but I prefer the pastes, as they create more vibrant, deep colors. Just a few drops of paste stirred into your

frosting in the buff go a long way. Ideally, you should own at minimum Red, Orange, Egg Yellow, Leaf Green, Sky or Royal Blue, Violet or Purple, Black, Brown or Chocolate Brown, and White. These are basics you can mix and match (see Chapter 4). One-ounce tubs of concentrated paste are available at most craft stores. They mix well and make beautiful colors, but they tend to have a bitter, metallic taste to them. The soft gel pastes are much harder to find, but I definitely prefer them because they are tasteless and blend well. The Internet or specialty kitchen and cake decorating stores are your best bet (see the resources listed at the end of this chapter). The 0.75-ounce bottles are fine for a few batches. If you are planning on making lots of cookies, go for the 4.5-ounce size. Some good brands that I've used: Ateco, Spectrum, Baker's Preferred, Americolor.

Parchment paper. I use parchment paper to line my baking trays for stick-free cookies, but if you use nonstick or greased trays, you won't need it. However, this item is on the absolutely necessary list, because you will first practice decorating on parchment paper.

Patience. This is very important, as learning to decorate cookies takes a bit of practice. The most time-consuming part is making frosting, mixing colors, and making bags. But stick with it!

Other

Scissors. You'll want a pair of scissors for cutting off the tips of decorating bags. Any size is fine.

Rubber bands. Keep a collection of rubber bands for tying off bags. You can use any size or width.

Toothpicks. You'll need these for unclogging tips.

Spatulas. You'll want a small one, for scraping mistakes off cookies, and larger ones for mixing colors. Stiff spatulas are best.

Containers and inexpensive bowls. Plastic, lidded storage containers are ideal, as you can mix and store frosting in the same container, and the frosting dye won't ruin your good bowls.

Optional, But Highly Recommended

You can still create fabulous cookies without the following supplies, but these items are useful to have handy.

Tip cleaner brush. You can also just soak the tips in sudsy water, but these little brushes, usually found in craft stores next to the tips, are a little easier. Be careful not to soak the tips too long lest they begin to rust.

Tip covers. When you're storing filled frosting bags, you can use these to cover the tips so the ends don't get chunky and clogged. However, if you'd like to conserve your money, little bits of plastic wrap also work well.

Cellophane favor bags and ribbon. If you plan on wrapping your cookies as gifts, these should be bumped up to the "absolutely necessary" list. See Chapter 8 for tips on how best to wrap your cookies.

All those other confusing contraptions you see—tips with stars and slits, thick pastry bags, wheels, tools with handles, presses—are utterly unnecessary for the projects in this book. Don't be confused by the many, many forms of frosting types and coloring out there: fondant, gum paste, dust, airbrushes, and lustres. Unless you know how to use them and specifically want to use them, don't worry about them. Stick with the concentrated paste or the soft gel paste (again, I recommend the latter).

Occasionally, edible glitters can make a nice addition; we often use them at the store to dress up Santa's beard, make glittery stars, or add sparkle to Dorothy's ruby slippers. I'll tell you how to use edible glitter when we get to decorating cookies. This glitter is optional, not to mention very expensive. But glitter can look beautiful, so if you prefer, use it once you feel comfortable with decorating.

Baker's Terms

Novice cookie decorators may need to learn some new lingo. Here are some common procedures and supplies—some terms may be familiar, but others may be new.

Almond extract: A concentrated flavoring made from bitter-almond oil and alcohol, widely used in pastries and baked goods. Found in the baking aisle of the supermarket. Imitation almond flavoring can be used as a substitute.

Buttercream Frosting: A creamy frosting made with softened butter, confectioners' sugar, milk, and sometimes flavoring.

Confectioners' sugar: The finest form of cane or beet sugar, also known as powdered sugar. Sometimes cornstarch is added to prevent caking.

Coupler: A two-piece, plastic device that includes a base and a ring that secures the tip and allows you to change the tip on a frosting bag.

Cream of tartar: A white, crystalline salt used in baking powder and to stabilize beaten egg whites. Found in the baking aisle of the supermarket.

Dragging: Holding the frosting bag too close to the cookie and using your decorating tip to push frosting. (This is a no-no.)

Granulated sugar: Common table sugar, meaning sugar in granules.

Knead: To work or press into a mass with the hands, folding over, pressing down, and turning.

Meringue powder: Powdered egg whites. Used to make Royal Icing. Found in the baking aisle of the supermarket, craft stores, and cake decorating supply stores.

Parchment paper: A silicone-based paper that can withstand high heat, often used in baking to prevent sticking.

Pipe: To squeeze frosting from a decorating bag in a controlled manner.

Rolled cookies: Cookies made from stiff dough that can withstand being rolled out and cut into shapes.

Royal Icing: A mixture of confectioners' sugar and egg whites that dries hard to the touch.

Vanilla extract: A vanilla-flavored product made by macerating chopped vanilla beans in a water-alcohol solution to extract the flavor. Found in the baking aisle of the supermarket. Imitation vanilla flavoring can be used as a substitute.

Resources

The Internet is an incredible tool. Using a search engine, type in "Cake Decorating Supplies" and your hometown. You might even have luck with "Cookie Decorating Supplies." You'll find a wealth of resources and stores that sell decorating bags, soft gel pastes, tips, couplers, and all of the other supplies you need.

Before You Buy

Copper cookie cutters are usually larger in size, between 4 and 7 inches, and are of the highest quality. They are a worthy investment, but much more expensive. Many of the tin or aluminum cutters are smaller, only 2 to 4 inches, but some do come in the larger size. When ordering cookie cutters online or over the phone, check how large they are and look at a ruler to envision the cutter. Often Web or catalog pictures can be deceiving, and you want to be sure to get a large enough cutter. You can still create beautiful cookies with miniature cutters, but detailed designs will be more difficult.

Finding cookie cutters at craft stores or specialty stores eliminates the mystery of online ordering. But the wonders of the Internet are many, as you can find just about any shape imaginable to match what you'd like to do, and you may not find such variety at a store.

Most of the supplies are available at craft stores. Tips, couplers, bags, brushes, and meringue powder are all easy to find. If you can buy locally, you'll have the advantage of avoiding shipping fees and not having to wait on shipments. Soft gel pastes are more difficult to find at a store, and Internet searches will help you find local suppliers. Still, at many stores, the color selection is limited. The Internet is a great resource to order soft gel pastes, but allow enough time for delivery before your event. In a pinch, concentrated gels, widely available from craft stores, can be used to great effect. I find they have a bitter aftertaste, so I prefer the soft gel pastes. Specialty food and kitchen stores also have many of the supplies you'll need, as well as good cookie cutter choices. Of course, your grocery store can supply parchment paper and most of the dough and frosting ingredients (even meringue powder!).

Sources for Decorating Supplies

The following resources are just a few of the many Internet suppliers and retail stores that offer decorating supplies and cookie cutters. Be sure to check the Web site for store locations and ordering information.

Craft Stores

A. C. Moore
www.acmoore.com

Jo-Ann Fabrics & Crafts
800-525-4951
www.joann.com

Michaels Arts and Craft Store
Michaels Stores, Inc.
Customer Service
8000 Bent Branch Drive
Irving, TX 75063
800-MICHAELS
www.michaels.com

Specialty Kitchen and Cooking Stores

Bridge Kitchenware
711 3rd Avenue
New York, NY 10017
212-688-4220
www.bridgekitchenware.com

Sur La Table
Seattle Design Center
5701 Sixth Avenue South, Suite 486
Seattle, WA 98108
800-243-0852 or
866-328-5412
www.surlatable.com

Williams-Sonoma
3250 Van Ness Avenue
San Francisco, CA 94109
877-812-6235
www.williamssonoma.com

More Great Stores
Call or visit the Web site first. Many
of these stores are Internet and catalog
only.

ABC Sugar Art
(wide selection of frosting color;
Internet only)
703-538-6222
www.abcsugarart.com

Americolor Corporation
(also a wide selection of frosting color;
Internet only, contact for ordering
information)
341 C Melrose Street
Placentia, CA 92870
800-556-0233
www.americolorcorp.com

Beryl's Cake Decorating and Pastry
Supplies
(lots of supplies, including frosting
color; Internet and catalog only)
PO Box 1584
North Springfield, VA 22151
703-256-6951
800-488-2749
www.beryls.com

Candyland Crafts
(supplies and cookie cutters)
201 West Main Street
Somerville, NJ 08876
908-685-0410
www.candylandcrafts.com

Country Kitchen SweetArt, Inc.
(great selection of frosting color)
4621 Speedway Drive
Fort Wayne, IN 46825
260-482-4835
800-497-3927
www.countrykitchensa.com

Fran's Cake and Candy Supplies
(great selection of supplies and
frosting color; retail location only)
Courthouse Plaza
10396 Willard Way
Fairfax, VA 22030
703-352-1471

House on the Hill, Inc.
(baking supplies and spectacular
replicas of historic cookie molds;
Internet and catalog only)
650 West Grand Avenue, Unit 110
Elmhurst, IL 60126
630-279-4455
www.houseonthehill.net

Kitchen Collectables
(nice selection of supplies and cutters;
Internet only)

8901 J Street, Suite 2
Omaha, NE 68127
888-593-2436
www.kitchengifts.com

Kitchen, Etc.
(baking supplies and cutters;
Internet only)
800-571-6316
www.kitchenetc.com

Sugarcraft, Inc.
(everything you'll need, including
frosting color; Internet only)
2715 Dixie Highway (Route 4)
Hamilton, OH 45015
www.sugarcraft.com

The Ultimate Baker
(more of everything you'll need,
including frosting color; Internet and
catalog only)
4917 East 2nd Avenue
Spokane Valley, WA 99212
866-285-2665
www.cooksdream.com

Wilton
(even more of everything you'll need;
Internet and catalog only)
Wilton Industries
2240 West 75th Street
Woodridge, IL 60517
630-963-1818
800-794-5866
www.wilton.com

Cookie Cutter Resources
The Cookie Cutter Shop
(Internet only)
Fax 360-652-3647
www.thecookiecuttershop.com

CopperGifts.com
(huge selection of copper cutters;
Internet only)
620-421-0654
www.coppergifts.com

H. O. Foose Tinsmithing Co.
18 West Poplar Street
Fleetwood, PA 19522
610-944-1960
www.foosecookiecutters.com

The Little Fox Factory
(nice selection of cookie cutters;
Internet only)
931 Marion Road
Bucyrus, OH 44820
419-562-5420
www.thelittlefoxfactory.com

If You Just Want to Buy 'Em
Bundles of Cookies
4930 Hampden Lane
Bethesda, MD 20814
301-652-8840
877-ON-A-STIK
www.bundlesofcookies.com

3

Your Dough and Your Frosting: The Bare Essentials

Before you begin to decorate, you must first create your canvas and your palette. This chapter will take you through Steps 1–3 of cookie decorating: making and chilling your cookie dough; rolling, cutting, and baking your shapes; and mixing your frosting. Getting the dough and the frosting exactly right will make learning to decorate cookies much easier. Frosting of a nice texture and perfect consistency is vital for decorated cookies, so a close reading of the instructions in this chapter is important. Any of your favorite recipes for rolled and cut-out cookies (or even store-bought dough) will work, but I've included recipes for sugar cookies, almond cookies, gingerbread cookies, and chocolate cookies that are tasty and easy to handle.

Your Dough: The Canvas

Baking cookies requires more than a great recipe. Learning the best way to prepare and manipulate your dough is just as important. Once you master the techniques for mixing, chilling, kneading, rolling, and cutting, you will be able to create the perfect cookie canvas.

Mixing. Most cookie dough is quite easy to handle. I usually blend with a standing mixer using the flat beater (as opposed to the wire whip), but you can use an electric hand mixer.

Chilling. Once mixed, you should always cover the dough with plastic wrap and chill in the refrigerator for about an hour, or at least thirty minutes if time is of the essence. A chilled-out dough will limit spreading and mushiness, so this is a vital step. If you over-chill to the point that the dough becomes hard (or if you make your dough a day or two in advance), let it sit out for an hour at room temperature.

Kneading. When your dough is ready and chilled, break off a third of the batch at a time and knead the dough until it is pliable and easy to manipulate. This should take only a few seconds! Try to minimize kneading, because an over-handled dough produces a tougher cookie.

Rolling. You'll need a floured surface and a rolling pin with a sleeve or a lightly floured rolling pin (the more flour you use, the tougher the cookie will taste, but don't skimp, as sticky cookies are a real hassle). Roll out about a third of the dough at a time, starting from the middle and working your way out, moving the dough clockwise a quarter-turn every few rolls to ensure the thickness is even. If the dough starts to crack, sprinkle some flour on the surface and press together with your fingers. Unlike pastry dough, this dough should roll out smoothly. If it cracks a lot, something went wrong. You may have added too much flour to the dough, or not enough liquid. Add a tablespoon of water, or wet your hands and knead the dough again.

Cutting. Most home-baked decorated cookies are thin, about one-eighth inch. I personally prefer a thicker, heartier cookie, about one-fourth to three-eighths of an inch. The gingerbread cookies tend to puff up a bit, however, so stick to one-eighth inch thick or only slightly thicker. Cut your shapes, reworking the dough as necessary, using cookie cutters or a sharp knife around a template (for the latter, smooth the edges with your fingers). Cut cookies as close together as possible to minimize handling of the dough. For cookie cutters with intricate shapes and little pieces prone to breakage, first dip the cutter in flour to help free the dough.

Baking. Place your cookies one to two inches apart on a baking sheet lined with parchment paper and bake in a fully preheated oven. Cool the sheets

Do I *have* to use "rolled" cookies?

The sugar cookie is commonly used for decorated cookies because it holds its shape well and the surface remains smooth. While you can decorate a chocolate chip cookie, the canvas is lumpy and bumpy. And the sweetness of the frosting tends to make the already sweet nature of the chocolate chip cookie unbearable (unless you really, really, really like sugar).

completely before setting the next batch on the pan, because cookies put on hot trays (or placed in an oven before it is preheated) are prone to spread. Between batches, keep the unused dough in the fridge until ready to cut and bake. None of the following recipes should spread if you follow these precautions.

Cookie Recipes

■ Sugar Cookies

4 cups all-purpose flour

½ teaspoon salt

1 teaspoon baking powder

1 cup (2 sticks) unsalted butter, slightly softened

2 cups granulated sugar

2 eggs

2 teaspoons vanilla extract

1 tablespoon water (optional)

Mix together and set aside the flour, salt, and baking powder. In a large bowl with an electric hand mixer or in the bowl of a standing mixer with a flat beater, cream the butter and sugar on medium speed. Beat in the eggs. Add the flour mixture and blend on low speed. Add the vanilla extract and blend. You may add a tablespoon of water if the dough feels dry.

Knead into a ball, cover with plastic wrap, and refrigerate for 30 minutes to 1 hour. Follow the previous directions for kneading, rolling, cutting, and baking.

Bake in a preheated 375° oven for 8 to 10 minutes for small cookies or 12 to 15 minutes for large cookies. The cookies are done when the edges are golden brown.

Yield: 12 to 16 large cookies (4 to 6 inches across) or 30 to 35 small cookies (2 to 3 inches across).

■ Almond Cookies

1 cup (2 sticks) salted, sweet cream butter, slightly softened

1 cup confectioners' sugar

1 egg

1½ teaspoons almond extract

1 teaspoon vanilla extract

2½ cups all-purpose flour

1 teaspoon salt

In a medium bowl with an electric hand mixer or in the bowl of a standing mixer with a flat beater, cream together the butter and confectioners' sugar. Add the egg, almond extract, and vanilla extract, and blend on medium speed. Mix in the flour and salt on low speed.

Knead into a ball, cover with plastic wrap, and refrigerate for 30 minutes to 1 hour. Follow the previous directions for kneading, rolling, cutting, and baking.

Bake in a preheated 375° oven for 15 to 20 minutes for large cookies or 12 to 15 minutes for small cookies. The cookies are done when the edges are golden brown.

Yield: 8 to 10 large cookies (4 to 6 inches across) or 20 to 25 small cookies (2 to 3 inches across).

■ Chocolate Cookies

1	cup (2 sticks) unsalted butter, slightly softened
1	cup granulated sugar
1	egg
1	teaspoon vanilla extract
2	cups flour
$\frac{1}{2}$	cup unsweetened cocoa powder
$\frac{1}{2}$	teaspoon baking soda
$\frac{1}{2}$	teaspoon salt

In a medium bowl with an electric hand mixer or in the bowl of a standing mixer with a flat beater, cream together the butter and sugar on medium speed. Add the egg and vanilla extract and blend on medium speed. Add the flour, cocoa powder, baking soda, and salt, and mix on low speed.

Knead into a ball, cover with plastic wrap, and refrigerate for 30 minutes to 1 hour. Follow the previous directions for kneading, rolling, cutting, and baking.

Bake in a preheated 375° oven for 12 to 14 minutes for large cookies or 10 to 12 minutes for small cookies. The cookies are done when the edges are golden brown.

Yield: 12 to 16 large cookies (4 to 6 inches across) or 30 to 35 small cookies (2 to 3 inches across).

■ Chocolate-Mint Cookies

Follow the recipe for Chocolate Cookies, but add $\frac{1}{2}$ teaspoon peppermint extract along with the vanilla extract.

■ Gingerbread Cookies

3   cups flour

1½   teaspoons baking powder

¾   teaspoon baking soda

¼   teaspoon salt

1   tablespoon ground ginger

2   teaspoons cinnamon

¼   teaspoon ground cloves

½   cup (1 stick) unsalted butter, slightly softened

¾   cup firmly packed dark brown sugar

1   egg

½   cup molasses

2   teaspoons vanilla extract

1   teaspoon grated orange peel (optional)

Mix together and set aside the flour, baking powder, baking soda, salt, ground ginger, cinnamon, and ground cloves. In a large bowl with an electric hand mixer or in the bowl of a standing mixer with a flat beater, cream together the butter and brown sugar on medium speed. Add and blend the egg, molasses, vanilla extract, and orange peel (if using). Gradually stir in the flour mixture.

Knead into a ball, cover with plastic wrap, and refrigerate for one hour. Follow the previous directions for kneading, rolling, cutting, and baking.

Bake in a preheated 375° oven for 10 to 12 minutes for large cookies or 8 to 10 minutes for small cookies. The cookies are done when the edges are golden brown.

Yield: 10 to 12 large cookies (4 to 6 inches across) or 25 to 30 small cookies (2 to 3 inches across).

Can my cookie cutter be used to make other shapes?

Always look at your cookie cutter from different perspectives—rotate it so the shape is upside down and sideways—because it can almost always be used for more designs than the one on the label. At the store, we use the mushroom cookie cutter for the beach umbrella and the scales of justice. The golf ball on a tee doubles as a stethoscope for a doctor or a blue ribbon for a marathon runner.

Your Frosting: The Palette

Frosting is the crucial element in a successfully decorated cookie. There is a confusing world of frosting types, terms, and techniques out there, and for every technique, the consistency and stiffness of frosting varies as well. Even if you're experienced with frosting, you'll want to read through this section to make sure you have the correct consistency for the techniques used here.

Buttercream Frosting versus Royal Icing

I suggest two types of frosting to decorate cookies: Buttercream Frosting and Royal Icing. (In this book, *icing* and *frosting* mean the same thing: the great, sugary stuff that will cover your cookies.) Buttercream Frosting is made primarily of butter, sugar, and milk, while Royal Icing is made primarily of egg whites, sugar, and water. Both Buttercream Frosting and Royal Icing have pros and cons.

I find that Buttercream Frosting tastes much better—and with a creamy, rich, butter base, how can it not? A downside of Buttercream, however, is that, because it includes milk and butter, it does not keep far beyond the day of decorating your cookies. You may refrigerate the frosting, but doing so will harden it beyond practical use.

Royal Icing is fabulous from an artistic standpoint. Royal Icing dries hard, which makes it ideal for giving decorated cookies as gifts, because you can wrap and pack them without smushing your labors of love. Buttercream will set if left overnight, but not as firmly as Royal Icing. I add some flavor and texture to the Royal Icing recipe to improve the taste and to allow some semblance of softness. You are not using the frosting as a glue, as in making a gingerbread house, so it is not necessary that it dry rock hard.

While fresh egg whites are traditionally used to make Royal Icing, meringue powder is a popular alternative. I use meringue powder to make Royal Icing rather than fresh egg whites. Meringue powder whips up nicely and a container stretches a lot farther than a carton of eggs. And with meringue powder as a base, you don't need to refrigerate your frosting or cookies, which makes storage much easier. With the popularity of cake and cookie decorating nowadays, meringue powder can be found at many supermarkets and in most craft stores that sell cake and cookie supplies.

Is my frosting too thick or too thin?

The frosting consistency cake decorators use when making three-dimensional flowers and designs is too thick. Thin it with some water. On the flip side, the frosting used when "flooding" (the process of piping a stiff frosting outline, then squeezing very fluid frosting on the cookie and letting it spread on its own to cover the cookie) is too thin. The thinner the frosting, the smoother the finished cookie looks, but the downside is the lack of control. Even though you might see some evidence of the piped lines when using the frosting consistency recommended in this book, the thicker frosting gives you so many more possibilities for decorating. Runny frosting is just too difficult to work with. Frosting that is "just right" should be halfway between the stiff consistency used in cake decorating and the liquid consistency used in flooding.

To improve the taste and texture of traditional Royal Icing to better match that of Buttercream, I add vegetable shortening. Vegetable shortening does not have to be refrigerated, as the butter and milk in Buttercream do. Adding shortening is not necessary, but your icing will be stiffer and less creamy without it. Shortening also cuts the super-sugary taste nicely. That being said, most of the recipe *is* sugar, and it will taste sugary no matter what. Don't panic if you miscount a tablespoon or two of water or if you spill in an extra half teaspoon of vanilla extract, as you won't taste much of a difference! Making frosting is really quite forgiving.

> ### Oh no! I ran out of sugar!
> Make sure you purchase enough confectioners' sugar. The Buttercream Frosting recipe calls for one sixteen-ounce box, but you should have another box handy in case you need more for thickening.

Yields

Pay attention to the yields! A nice-sized bag of frosting is about $3/4$ cup. The Royal Icing recipe yields 4 cups, or about six bags of frosting. The Buttercream Frosting yields only $2\frac{1}{4}$ cups of frosting, enough for three to four bags of frosting. You may need more than one batch, but as Buttercream is not conducive to storage, it's best to work in smaller amounts. Portion out your frosting before adding color. Depending on what you need, you can make more or less of a color. For example, if you are outlining in black, make only $1/2$ cup of black, but double or triple your fill-in color. For large projects, especially if this is your first time decorating and you need some practice time, you may want to make a couple of batches of Buttercream. One batch of Royal Icing should make enough to decorate all the cookies in any of the above cookie recipes—and leave you with some practice frosting and even some leftovers.

Consistency, Consistency, Consistency

Many factors affect your frosting consistency, including heat, humidity, and the frosting's mood. If your frosting is much too runny, it will be difficult to work with. If it's much too stiff, it'll be too tough to get out of the bag.

The consistency should be like a very thick milkshake. After you've mixed the frosting according to the recipe, take a dollop of frosting in your spoon and turn it upside down. The frosting should cling to the spoon for several seconds before slowly falling back into the bowl.

If the consistency isn't right, to thicken runny frosting, add one large spoonful of confectioners' sugar at a time. Add one teaspoon at a time of water to thin Royal

Icing, or one teaspoon of milk at a time to thin Buttercream Frosting, until the perfect consistency is reached.

There is a window within which you can work. You don't need to get the measurements to just the right grain of sugar and drop of water or milk. Remember Steps 8 and 9 of cookie decorating: piping the outline of your design with frosting, letting it set, and filling in the design with frosting. If the frosting's a little too runny, you just have to make sure your outline is good and set before you fill in, and on the plus side, the finished look is nice and smooth. If it's a little too stiff, you can still work with it, but you'll just see the "lines" of the frosting more when you go to fill in your design.

When in doubt, slightly stiffer is better than too runny. When making colors, the frosting dye tends to make the icing runnier. It's much more difficult to make frosting stiffer once it's blended, as confectioners' sugar tends to add lumps that can clog tips. If you do add more sugar, you may want to sift it first. Or stir very, *very* well.

Frosting (in the Buff) Recipes

Frosting in the buff is your starter frosting. To make any color, including white, dye must be added to the Royal Icing or the Buttercream Frosting (see Chapter 4).

■ Royal Icing

½   cup water

4   tablespoons meringue powder

5 to 7 cups confectioners' sugar (see notes)

½   teaspoon cream of tartar (optional; see notes)

½   cup vegetable shortening

1 to 2 teaspoons vanilla extract (optional, but recommended)

In a large bowl with an electric hand mixer or in the bowl of a standing mixer with a wire whip, blend the water and meringue powder on low speed. Once the ingredients are blended, change to the highest speed and whip the mixture. Work through the foamy stage until you have a thick, fluffy concoction and stiff peaks form when the beaters move through the mixture, at least 5 minutes.

Mix in the confectioners' sugar, cream of tartar, vegetable shortening, and vanilla extract. Start on the lowest setting and work your way up to a medium speed lest you get an ear, eye, mouth, and room full of powdered sugar!

Once the frosting is mixed, achieve the perfect consistency for decorating by adding confectioners' sugar to thicken or adding water to thin.

Yield: 4 cups of frosting, or about 6 frosting bags.

Notes: You may use more or less confectioners' sugar to achieve the desired consistency; as a 16-ounce box contains only about $3\frac{1}{2}$ cups, you'll need at least two boxes.

Cream of tartar is used to stabilize egg whites. Most meringue powder comes premixed with cream of tartar. Check the ingredients on the meringue powder container; if cream of tartar is included, you do not need to add it as a separate ingredient.

■ Buttercream Frosting

1   (16-ounce) box confectioners' sugar

$\frac{1}{2}$ cup (1 stick) salted, sweet cream butter, slightly softened

4 to 6 tablespoons milk

1   teaspoon vanilla extract

In a medium bowl using an electric hand mixer or in the bowl of a standing mixer with the flat beater, cream together the confectioners' sugar, butter, milk, and vanilla extract until well blended, on medium speed. Once the frosting is mixed, achieve the perfect consistency for decorating by adding confectioners' sugar to thicken or adding milk to thin.

Yield: $2\frac{1}{4}$ cups of frosting, or about 3 to 4 frosting bags.

4

Your Paints:
Mixing Colors and Making
Them Match

Now it's time to brighten up your frosting with beautiful colors. This chapter will walk you through Steps 4 and 5 of cookie decorating: dividing your frosting in the buff and mixing your frosting colors. Because of the breadth of the design possibilities, we will be working with a wide range of colors beyond the traditional food color kit (red, yellow, blue, and green). You can make just about any desired shade, based on your taste and need.

Dividing Your Frosting

Once you choose a cookie design, decide how many colors you will need and divide your frosting into small bowls. Remember, you should only need about ¾ cup of frosting for each color for one batch of cookies. But make a little more of the colors you will be using to fill in, and a little less for colors you will be using to outline your design. It's also a good idea to leave a little extra frosting in the buff in case you need more of a color once you start to decorate.

Creating Your Colors

Perfecting the mixing of colors is best done through trial and error.

These guidelines will help eliminate waste. I capitalized the names of colors most used by different companies to label their dye, though you may find slight variations (such as "Buttercup Yellow" versus "Egg Yellow").

As I noted in Chapter 2, the basic dye colors available are

1. Red
2. Orange
3. Egg Yellow
4. Leaf Green
5. Sky or Royal Blue
6. Violet or Purple
7. Black
8. Brown or Chocolate Brown
9. White

While Red, Orange, Purple, Black, and White are pretty consistent, other colors come in several variations. I rarely use the Lemon Yellow, because to me it appears fluorescent and unappetizing. Egg Yellow is a much preferred alternative. However, if you like the neon glow of Lemon Yellow, by all means try it.

Leaf Green is versatile and easy to mix with other colors, and I prefer it to Forest Green. Forest Green pretty much makes only an evergreen color, while Leaf Green can be used in chartreuse, bright green, or mint green, and it works well matched with almost any other color. Besides, you can make Forest Green from Leaf Green by adding a drop of Royal Blue.

You have a choice between Sky Blue and Royal Blue. Sky Blue works well for baby boy cookies and pastels, but for darker blues or to mix with other colors (such as Purple, to create cornflower), Royal Blue is preferred.

If you become serious about decorating or have a particular project in mind, other colors may be useful, such as Burgundy, Pink (Soft or Electric), Forest Green, and Peach. I highly recommend adding them to your collection. Fuchsia, Copper, Teal, and Turquoise are just a few of the many other shades available that I don't own, but come in handy from time to time.

The following guidelines offer vague amounts because variables are so unpredictable, such as dye brand, concentration, and the amount of frosting used.

You really need to play around with the amount of dye to get the exact color you want.

Always, always, always start with one drop and add one at a time. One drop of frosting color goes a long way. It's much easier to add color than to take it away. However, if you do go too far, you can add more frosting in the buff or even White dye, but be warned that the white will affect the color.

I add White on purpose to make colors more pastel and iridescent, such as in making light pink, lavender, baby yellow, mint, or baby blue. Also remember, if using the soft gel paste, the more color you add, the runnier your frosting will be. Colors such as white, red, black, royal blue, forest green, and dark purple take a lot of gel paste and are often victims of runniness. You may need to add some sifted powdered sugar.

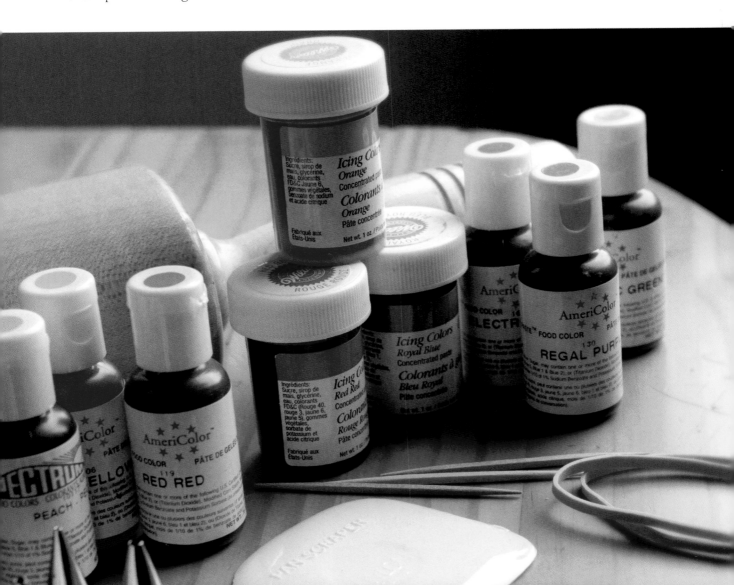

You might want to bookmark the following guidelines for quick reference when you start mixing. Refer to Color Chart 1 on page 34 to see what the colors should look like.

Red: Many, many drops of Red

Burgundy: Many drops of Burgundy and a couple drops of Red to get rid of the purplish tinge, or lots of drops of Red and one or two drops of Purple or even Brown

Light pink: One or two drops of Pink and a couple drops of White. I use Electric Pink for all shades of pink, even the lightest, because it appears much brighter. But you may also use Soft Pink for all shades if you prefer a more muted look.

Medium pink: A few drops of Pink

Hot pink: Lots of drops of Pink ("Electric Pink" really preferred here)

Peach: A few drops of Peach or a drop of Orange with a drop of Egg Yellow

Orange: Several drops of Orange

Burnt orange: Lots of drops of Orange

Baby yellow: A couple drops of Egg Yellow and a few drops of White

Butter yellow: A few drops of Egg Yellow

Gold: Lots of drops of Egg Yellow

Mint green: One or two drops of Leaf or Forest Green and a few drops of White

Light slime green (or light chartreuse, also known as light lime): A couple drops of Leaf Green, a drop or two of Egg Yellow, and a drop or two of White

Slime green (chartreuse or lime): A couple drops of Leaf Green, a couple drops of Egg Yellow. (*Note:* Some brands now carry an Electric Green, which is a very nice, premixed Egg Yellow and Leaf Green.)

Bright green: Lots of drops of Leaf Green

Forest green: Lots and lots of Leaf Green and a drop of Royal Blue, or to really look forest-like, you can buy Forest Green

Baby blue: A couple drops of Sky Blue and a few drops of White

Bright blue: A few drops of Sky Blue

Royal blue: Many drops of Royal Blue

Cornflower: A couple drops of Royal Blue, a couple drops of Violet or Purple

Lavender: One or two drops of Violet or Purple, a few drops of White

Medium purple: A few drops of Violet or Purple

Dark purple: A lot more drops of Violet or Purple

Caucasian flesh: One or two drops of Peach, and can add one drop of Egg Yellow

Light brown: A few drops of Brown, often named Chocolate Brown; if it looks too pink, add one drop Egg Yellow

Medium brown: Lots of drops of Brown or Chocolate Brown

Dark brown: Lots more drops of Brown or Chocolate Brown

Light gray: A couple drops of Black, a few drops of White

Medium gray: A few drops of Black, a few drops of White

Black: *Lots* of drops of Black

White: *Lots* of drops of White. Remember, because frosting in the buff tends to have a yellow or brown tint to it, to make white frosting you need White dye!

Color Chart 1: Colors to Create with Your Frosting Dye

Red	Baby blue
Burgundy	Bright blue
Light pink	Royal blue
Medium pink	Cornflower
Hot pink	Lavender
Orange	Medium purple
Burnt orange	Dark purple
Peach	Caucasian flesh
Baby yellow	Light brown
Butter yellow	Medium brown
Gold	Dark brown
Mint green	Light gray
Light slime green	Gray
Slime green	Black
Bright green	White
Forest green	

For guidance in choosing colors that work well together, see Color Chart 2. The chart shows attractive combinations and offers suggestions for fill-in and out-line colors.

Color Chart 2: Colors That Work Well Together

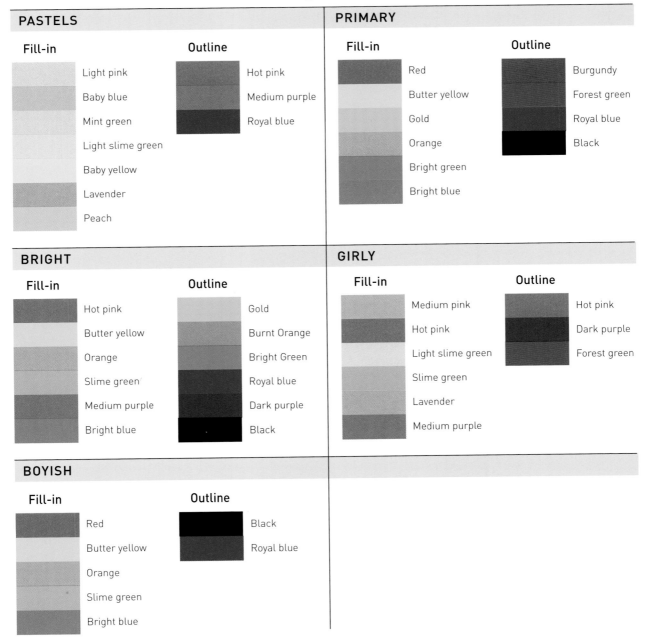

PASTELS

Fill-in	Outline
Light pink	Hot pink
Baby blue	Medium purple
Mint green	Royal blue
Light slime green
Baby yellow
Lavender
Peach

PRIMARY

Fill-in	Outline
Red	Burgundy
Butter yellow	Forest green
Gold	Royal blue
Orange	Black
Bright green
Bright blue

BRIGHT

Fill-in	Outline
Hot pink	Gold
Butter yellow	Burnt Orange
Orange	Bright Green
Slime green	Royal blue
Medium purple	Dark purple
Bright blue	Black

GIRLY

Fill-in	Outline
Medium pink	Hot pink
Hot pink	Dark purple
Light slime green	Forest green
Slime green
Lavender
Medium purple

BOYISH

Fill-in	Outline
Red	Black
Butter yellow	Royal blue
Orange
Slime green
Bright blue

Choosing the Colors for Your Design

For the designs in this book, I indicate the colors and tip sizes you will need for outlining and filling in, but for when you break away on your own, here are some good rules of thumb for color choices:

- Outline in black or dark gray and fill in with the above color sets or outline in a darker color (such as burgundy, burnt orange, evergreen or bright green, royal blue, or dark purple) and fill in with a lighter version of the *same* color.
- If making pastel cookies, outline in a darker, medium color (such as medium purple, hot pink, slime or bright green, bright blue, or gold) and fill in with the light version of the same color.
- *Never* (or rarely, depending on your taste) outline in a light color and fill in with a darker version of the same color. In fact, I've only used light colors for outlining in a few rare cases when I've filled with the same color. I just don't like the way light colors look for outlines.

Yikes! My good china is ruined!

While for the most part, frosting dyes are easy to clean and don't usually stain, the dyes that contain red (including Burgundy, Red, of course, Purple, and Black) are the absolute cruelest. If you get some dye on your hands, it may stay there until time wears it away. When using these red-based colors (or any color, to be safe), clean bowls and utensils quickly. Don't let the frosting sit in your dishes for days or you will have a colorful surprise. Mixing in plastic storage containers or using spoons and spatulas you won't mind staining is ideal just in case some frosting color lingers. Don't wear your favorite outfit to decorate, and do not use your grandmother's china for mixing!

5

Your Tools: Bags of Frosting and Tips on Tips

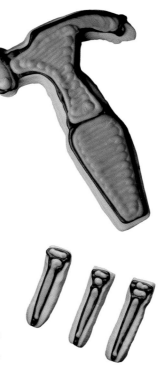

You've mixed your colors, so now it's time to get your cookie decorating tools ready. In this chapter you will master Steps 6 and 7, assembling and filling your frosting bag. We'll pay special attention to selecting the right tip. The Tip Chart might be a good place for a bookmark until you decorate so many cookies that picking up the right-sized tip becomes second nature. (By then, you'll be able to tell what size a tip is just by glancing at it, rather than reading the number on the side!)

Assembling the Decorating Bag

The wall of mysterious tools and trinkets in the cake decorating supply stores or the baker's aisle of your craft store may seem overwhelming, but really, cookie decorating requires only a few simple, inexpensive items: For each bag of frosting, all you need is a twelve-inch clear plastic decorating bag, a coupler, a tip, and a rubber band. Oh, and the frosting!

1. Open the wide end of a decorating bag and fold over to form a cuff.
2. Take a coupler and unscrew the ring.

step 1

steps 2, 3, and 4

steps 5 and 6

3. Place the coupler without the ring inside the bag, with the narrow end of the coupler closest to the pointed end of the decorating bag.

4. With scissors, snip off the pointed end of the decorating bag, about ½ inch. The cut edge of the bag should extend at least several millimeters past the end of the coupler or else the frosting will ooze out the sides. The coupler should be completely inside the bag.

5. Take a decorating tip in the size that you need, and place it over the cut end of the bag and hold onto the coupler's edge.

6. Take the ring, slide it over the tip, and screw it onto the coupler, securing the tip. Thus, the ring is outside the bag and the coupler is inside the bag, which might feel awkward with the plastic decorating bag in between, like catching your shirt in your zipper!

Filling the Bag

Depending on the number of colors you need and how much you'll need of each color (for outlining colors, fill the bag a bit less; for filling-in colors, fill the bag a bit more), an average bag should hold about ¾ cup of frosting.

Once you've assembled the bag, place the bag in a tall tumbler or small vase (a plastic tumbler or vase is ideal as it won't break), so the tip is inside, toward the bottom of the tumbler. Fold the wide end of the frosting bag over the tumbler's edges. Remember, we already folded over this end to insert the coupler. Scoop the frosting into the bag using a spoon or a spatula. Depending on how much frosting you have, fill the bag anywhere from half full to a maximum of three-fourths full. Don't fill it to the top of the bag as this will make piping the frosting too difficult, and don't get too much frosting at the top of the bag around the folded area as this will make your hands messy later! Carefully remove the bag from the tumbler or vase, unfold the top, twist the bag right above the top of the frosting, and wrap a rubber band *tightly* around the twisted bag.

What Your Tips Mean

You should have several of the round tips: sizes 1, 2, 3, 4, 5, and 6. Relatively speaking, these simple tips are considered small. You might see big tips in the store with stars, curves, slits, and other shapes that create big, three-dimensional designs. These fancy tips may be great for decorating thick designs on large cakes, but they are unnecessary for cookies. Our cookie world is smaller in scale and only two-dimensional (that is, nice and flat and great for packaging), but just as beautiful.

Now, what do you do with your tips? Which do you use for what? As you grow accustomed to handling the frosting bag and as you learn what comes out of each tip and what you can do with it, you'll pick and choose the tips that work best for you. But here are the guidelines:

■ Tip Chart

Size 1: Fine detail

You'll hardly use this at all until you become more expert. This is a tiny tip used when you need a pencil-sized accent such as the glint in the eye of a cartoon character. Hold off on purchasing this tip until you feel totally comfortable with decorating. It can be tough to control such a small line of frosting, and it isn't always easy to squeeze frosting out of such a tiny tip with consistency.

Size 2: Details

This is also a small tip, but easier to manage. It's the "finisher" tip, great for accents on top of the decorated cookie. Use it to draw swirls and dots on a wedding cake or dress, to put a smiley face on a person, to form a pig's curly tail, for writing, and so on.

Size 3: Outlining and writing

This is a great smallish-but-substantial tip—an absolute must-have. It's perfect for outlining your design or for writing a big, loopy name on top of a cookie. It's small enough to manage the frosting without its pouring out everywhere, but big enough to let the frosting come out nicely and consistently. Sometimes I even use a 3 tip to fill in a small space.

Size 4: Outlining and filling in

The 4 is a good middle-of-the-road tip. It's

great for the moderate, noncommittal type of decorator. For simpler designs where you don't need as much room to draw, it's great for outlining (the bigger the outline, the less it gets lost when filling in). But it's also good if you don't have that much to fill in.

Sizes 5 and 6: Filling in

Both of these big tips are great for filling in. If you are pinching pennies, you can buy just the 5 and forgo the 6, but if you have lots of wide-open spaces, your hands will thank you for using the 6. It's just a smidgeon bigger than the 5, but you can still feel the difference. Because these tips are the biggest, the frosting will be the thickest, so cookies decorated with these tips take the longest to dry. You wouldn't want to outline with these tips, because the fat lines of frosting would be too hard to manage. But they do great for fillin'.

Now for the Fun Part: Decorating!

Finally we arrive at the fun part—decorating. This chapter will explain Steps 8, 9, and 10, the basics of cookie design: drawing the design, filling in the outlined design, and adding the details. Along the way, you'll also learn how to hold the bag, how to stop a line of frosting, how to fix mistakes, and much more.

Know How to Hold 'Em . . .

Assemble a bag with a 4 tip in any color you wish. Once your bag is assembled, filled, and rubber banded, you're ready to begin. Nervous? Don't worry, we'll practice on parchment paper until you're comfortable enough to face your cookie canvas.

For all the righties out there, with your right hand, place your thumb and index finger around the bag so the frosting sits in your palm, as though the frosting bag is a pen. This works best when the bag is only half full, so you aren't grabbing more than you can hold comfortably. Even with a partially full bag, I often twist the bag around the center and only hold the lower half for the best control. Thus, the ring formed by my index finger and thumb sits either around the

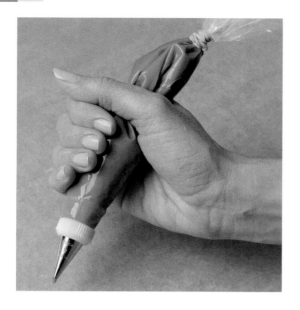

rubber band, or, for a fuller bag, at the center of the bag, twisted to divide the bag in half.

This right hand will be the force behind all the decorating, the power, the center, the be-all and end-all, the root of the aches and pains at the end of the day. Rest your left hand on top of your right. While the left hand doesn't have much power, keeping your hands together helps steady things so your lines come out nice and strong without wavering.

For lefties, the instructions on how to hold your hand comfortably are pretty much the same, but you will hold the bag with your left hand, squeeze and direct with your left hand, and rest your right hand on the bag to steady it.

Cookie Art: The Secret

Before the decorating begins, squeeze your decorating hand until some frosting comes out of the tip. I *always* squeeze the first bit out onto the table or a napkin whenever I start any cookie and whenever I change color. Needless to say, by the end of the day, I have a big pile of frosting bits.

Practice piping lines on your parchment paper. By "piping," I mean that you want to squeeze the bag with steady and controlled pressure from the decorating hand (right for righties, left for lefties). Keep your bag at a forty-five degree angle

to the paper, just as you would with a pen, and do *not* touch your tip to the paper or cookie. "Dragging" makes for a very messy-looking cookie. Your tip should hover about an eighth to a quarter of an inch above the paper. The only times your tip should either touch or come close to the paper (and later, the cookie) are when you start and finish outlining your design or filling in with frosting. To end, push the tip down, give an extra squeeze, and pull away quickly. Ending without little dollops and peaks or without pulling the frosting with you is a challenge and will need quite a bit of practice. I still mess this up on occasion!

Once you've mastered the line, turn to the Practice

Pages in Chapter 7. You may use the parchment paper and pipe the shapes while referring to the template as a guide, or you may place parchment paper directly over the template page. For a nice flat surface, scan or copy the page to a sheet of paper, then place a piece of parchment over the paper.

Outline and Fill

Now we've arrived at the final steps and the most challenging part of the process: decorating the cookie. First you need to learn the basic technique of outlining your design with frosting and filling in with frosting.

On your parchment paper, start with the squares.

1. Pipe the outline of a square on the parchment using a 3 or 4 tip in any color. Begin at the top left corner and pipe all four sides with one continuous line. Bring the tip closer to the parchment at the four corners to help you define the corners, but don't stop piping until you finish your square. Keep squeezing! End at the top left corner, using the technique you used earlier for ending (push the tip downward, give a little extra squeeze, and pull away quickly). This is your outline.

2. Let the outline set for about ten minutes. During this time, you can continue to practice outlining more squares.

3. With a 4 or 5 tip in any color, re-outline the design just inside the set line. This is for the sake of appearance, so the filled-in frosting won't have choppy edges; it gives you a cleaner-looking cookie.

4. Starting at the top left corner of the square with the same bag of color (or, if easier for lefties, starting at the top right corner), pipe the frosting back and forth continuously, one line under another, from left to right, right to left, left to right, and so on, until you reach the bottom of the square. Try not to stop squeezing until you fill the square completely. Don't stop and start your lines; you need to keep piping in a zigzag, continuous motion. Make sure you extend each back-and-forth piped line to touch the sides of the square and to entirely fill the space. You don't want to leave any gaps or holes.

Ouch! My hand hurts!

You know your frosting is too thick when you have to squeeze the life out of the bag to get it out (or when the bag bursts, covering your hands with gooey, sticky frosting). If this is the case, no worries. Remove the tip and squeeze the contents of the bag into a bowl. One teaspoon at a time, add tap water and stir until you get just the right consistency. Then refill the bag with the thinner frosting.

This outline-and-fill technique will be the building block of *all* your decorating. Don't be surprised if it takes a while to get the hang of it, even if you think it looks easy. The technique does get a little complicated when working with complex shapes with tight corners and crevices. For example, when decorating a palm tree, you don't have big blocks of space that give you room to go back and forth. Yet, I still use the same technique. I outline the palm tree, then go back and fill with color. I don't necessarily stick with back and forth; I tend to just get creative with squeezing frosting in where it fits. You might have to stop and start several times to fill all the spots.

Once you finish the squares, practice the same technique with the other shapes. Then practice the swirls and dots with a 2 and 3 tip, to get the feel of what each tip offers. You can also practice writing. For short words on a large cookie, the 3 tip works best. For a longer message on a smaller cookie, stick with the 2 tip.

We All Make Mistakes

Here are some things that may go wrong and some suggestions for fixing them.

Holes in the frosting. Holes and gaps are inevitable. There is just no way to draw perfectly straight lines without computer assistance. When you pipe one line under another to fill in a color, the lines of frosting may not line up exactly. And when you have odd shapes to fill, it may be difficult to keep a consistent back-and-forth motion, so you may leave a nagging space with bare cookie peeking through. The easy answer—going back and sticking a miniature line over the hole—tends to look the worst (though I admit I have been guilty of doing this). You also don't want to "drag" the tip, using it to push frosting into the gap. Messy, messy, messy. The best way of dealing with the problem is to keep going. Continue piping back and forth. When you get below the hole, use a bit of extra squeezing pressure to "push" the newly piped frosting up against the frosting above it; this will shove frosting into the space.

Shaky lines. Your lines are shaky because you're new to decorating. Aside from not having built up the hand muscles yet, you are moving slowly and carefully to make sure the technique is right. Once you gain expertise and confidence, you will move your hands more quickly and not worry as much about doing things correctly. The swifter movement will take care of the shaky lines.

Running out of steam. Not all of us have Hulk-like hands. You may tire halfway through filling the cookie or your bag may run out of frosting. No problem. Just stop by using the technique practiced earlier for ending (push the tip down, squeeze, and pull away quickly), rest your hand, gather up some frosting, and begin again. You'll likely notice the stop-and-start mark, but remember that these are cookies—not Fabergé eggs! Little marks of imperfection are completely okay. Your finished product will still be fabulous.

Edible Glitter, as Promised

If you decide to use edible glitter, decorate as you would ordinarily, but sprinkle some glitter over the section you want to sparkle right after you pipe the frosting. You must add the glitter while the frosting is wet or it won't stay on the cookie. Using glitter that matches the frosting color tends to look the best. If you only want part of your cookie covered with glitter, decorate this part first, add the glitter, turn the cookie over quickly to shake off the excess, then finish decorating the cookie. Again, while glitter is a beautiful embellishment to a cookie, the dear cost of the stuff makes it a little less than practical.

To Save Some Time

If after a long day of decorating cookies you find yourself weary (but still have twenty cookies to go), you can always resort to the quick decorating method. Simply cut out your cookies, bake, and let cool. Outline and fill the shape with a solid color, let set, and decorate whimsical designs (such as stripes, dots, or swirls) on top with a 2 tip. (This method is much quicker than drawing a complicated design on a cookie and filling in each section.) This technique works best using cookie cutters with distinct shapes that are easy to recognize without a detailed design (such as numbers or letters, shapes, flowers, animals, etc.). If you pick up a cookie cutter and don't know right away what it is supposed to be, this method won't work. It still

Aagghh! My frosting is running everywhere!

You know you've gone too far with the water when your frosting starts to run off the side of the cookie. I've scraped many a cookie in utter frustration when my beautiful design ended up a blended mess spilling off onto the table. Remove the tip and squeeze the contents of the bag back into the bowl. Gradually add *sifted* powdered sugar and mix until the frosting stiffens up a bit. You might need to add a whole cup if you really went overboard with the water. Place the thickened frosting in the bag and try again.

Help! The frosting is trapped in the bag!

Those are just big lumps of sugar blocking the way. First, take a toothpick and dig into the tip from the opening. This should break up the sugar enough for you to squeeze out the pieces onto a napkin. If this doesn't work, you'll have to remove the whole tip from the coupler and dig the toothpick around from the wider end. This should solve the problem.

makes a big hit to decorate several cookies with a detailed design and the rest with just this whimsical method.

Clean Up and Storage

When the cookies are done, what do you do with all of your supplies and leftover ingredients? If you plan on decorating cookies frequently, you might want to purchase some good, airtight storage bins for your cookie cutters, tips, couplers, and leftover frosting.

Clean your cutters with mild detergent and let them dry completely before storing. Food particles may attract critters or invite mold. The same goes for your tips. Let your tips soak in soapy water for about thirty minutes, and then scrub them with a tip brush. Do not let your tips soak too long or they will rust. Rinse them and let them dry fully before storing.

Plastic lidded containers are great for storing leftover frosting, though the colors may stain the insides. Buttercream Frosting will not keep past the day or two that you use it for decorating, because refrigeration will harden the frosting. So while it tastes divine because of the milk and butter, Buttercream is not a good choice if you plan on saving some frosting.

Royal Icing made with meringue powder will keep for several weeks without refrigeration. Keep unused frosting in airtight containers or the top will get a layer of crust. You can also keep bags of frosting. I recommend purchasing tip covers for the ends, but you can also use little pits of plastic wrap and rubber bands to seal the tip's end. After a while, the frosting will begin to break down and become sticky and gross, so you should use it within a few weeks.

Unused dough can be wrapped tightly and refrigerated for a couple of days. Let it sit at room temperature about an hour before using to allow the dough to soften enough to manipulate.

7

Templates and Designs:
Unique Ideas from Aliens to Worms

I n this chapter, you'll find templates and design ideas for cookies that we've created at Bundles of Cookies. After you choose a cookie design, practice on parchment paper first with the tip size and colors suggested before moving on to the real, live cookie. You can always scrape the frosting off the cookie if you make a mistake, though it may leave a "stain" on the cookie surface. The stains will be hidden by the finished cookie, but after three or four scrapes, the marks might confuse you when you try to pipe a design. You can use the same method as with the Practice Pages, of either mimicking the design freehand on parchment paper or copying or scanning the template and placing parchment paper over the piece of paper.

How to Use the Templates

Each cookie design will be accompanied by a list of the colors and tips you need as well as two or three drawings at the end of the chapter:

■ The first drawing is simply the outline of the cookie cutter so you have a sense of what the bare cookie looks like.

- The next drawing shows the basic frosting outline. Mimic the outline as closely as possible using the colors and tip sizes indicated, but don't worry if your version doesn't exactly match the template. Your hand will naturally adapt the design to your own style. Following the steps, fill in with the colors and tip sizes indicated.
- The final picture shows the finished cookie. Most designs have details done on top of the finished, filled-in cookie. The cookie should be filled in completely and set for several minutes before piping the details on top, usually with a 2 tip. The steps will indicate when this is necessary with the heading "Details."

Note: For cookies with no details on top, such as the baby carriage, shell, bee, butterfly, and daisy, the second drawing *is* your finished cookie. For simpler cookies, such as the letters, the heart, or the snowflake, the outline of the cookie cutter *is* your basic frosting outline, so you will also only see *two* drawings. Outline the shape just inside the edge of the cookie. Fill in the outlined shape with the colors and tip sizes indicated, and add your details on top of the filled-in cookie once the frosting has set.

About Cookie Cutters

There are hundreds, if not thousands, of cookie cutter shapes out there, but among different companies, there is a surprising consistency. If you search for a lobster cookie cutter, for example, you might find a hundred cookie cutters, but they will all have a similar shape. For most of the following designs, you can find an appropriate cutter from many of the suggested resources in Chapter 2 or from your own resources, so you don't need to shop anywhere in particular.

Also, you are not limited to following the templates precisely, so the designs can translate to similarly shaped cutters if you are using ones that are not exactly the same size or outline.

And lastly, if you do not want to purchase tons of cookie cutters to use only once or twice, you can use the templates I provide and cut out the cookies by hand. Hold

How long do I wait for the frosting to set?

After you draw your outline, let the frosting set for at least ten minutes, because filling in will be easier if you do, I promise. Many details (such as faces and writing) are done on top of the filled-in cookie with a smaller 2 tip. Fill in the large spaces, let the frosting set for ten to fifteen minutes, and pipe the detail on top. Designs will indicate when this step is necessary.

a thin sheet of paper over the book page, trace the design with a marker, and cut it out with scissors. If you would like to enlarge or minimize the design, you can do so with a scanner or a copy machine before cutting out. Most cookie cutters range from a small, 2 to 4 inch size (usually aluminum) to a larger 5 to 6 inch size (usually copper). By making cookies any larger, you run the risk of having a mushy, undercooked, and breakable center.

To use the paper template to cut your cookies, place it over rolled-out cookie dough and cut around the paper with a knife. Smooth the edges of the cookie with your fingers before baking. The template-cutting method will inevitably leave some rough spots along the sides, and if you have many to cut out, this method is time-consuming. Cookie cutters are faster and easier, but this is an alternative.

As we boast at the store, "we can do anything on a cookie," so occasionally customers challenge us with designs for which no cookie cutter exists, such as a specific corporate logo, cartoon characters, or a T-bone steak with a baked potato side. These we cut out by hand.

Know Your ABCs

Letters and Numbers

(See templates on page 90.)

You'll need:

4 tip bright green

5 tip slime green

2 tip medium pink

Note: You may substitute any bright color to outline, a lighter version of the same color to fill in, and any variety of bright colors for decoration.

1. Outline cookie with 4 tip bright green. Let set.
2. Fill in with 5 tip slime green.

Details:

3. When set, pipe swirls and dots with 2 tip pink.

Space Invaders

Spaceship
(See templates on page 90.)

You'll need:
3 and 2 tip black
3 tip orange
4 and 3 tip white
4 and 2 tip gray
3 tip slime green
3 tip gold

1. Outline design with 3 tip black. Let set.
2. Outline flames with 3 tip orange. Let set.
3. Fill in space ship with 4 tip white and 4 tip gray.
4. Fill in alien with 3 tip slime green. Let set.
5. Fill in window background with 3 tip black.
6. Fill in flames with 3 tip gold.

Details:

7. Pipe dots on spaceship body with 2 tip gray.
8. Pipe two dots for eyes with 3 tip white. Let set.
9. Pipe two dots in the white eyes and the rest of smiley face with 2 tip black.

Under the Sea

Fish

(See templates on page 91.)

You'll need:
3 and 2 tip black
4 tip butter yellow
4 or 5 tip slime green
4 tip bright blue
3 tip white

Note: You may substitute any bright colors.

1. Outline design with 3 tip black. Let set.
2. Fill in fish face and fins with 4 tip yellow. Let set.
3. Fill in body with 4 or 5 tip slime green. Let set.
4. Fill in tail with 4 tip bright blue.

Details:

5. Pipe big dot for eye with 3 tip white. Let set.
6. Pipe dot in white to make an eye, pipe mouth, and pipe scales with 2 tip black.

Octopus

(See templates on page 91.)

You'll need:
3 tip black
5 tip bright blue
3 tip baby blue
3 tip white
2 tip royal blue

1. Outline design with 3 tip black. Let set.
2. Fill in octopus with 5 tip bright blue. Let set.
3. Fill in under tentacles with 3 tip baby blue. Let set.

Details:

4. Pipe white dots for eyes with 3 tip white. Let set.
5. Pipe dots in white for eyes with 3 tip black.
6. Pipe dots on tentacles and two lines between eyes with 2 tip royal blue.

A Day at the Beach

Palm Tree

(See templates on page 92.)

You'll need:

3 tip dark brown

3 tip forest green

4 tip medium brown

4 or 5 tip bright green

1. Outline tree trunk in 3 tip dark brown. Let set.
2. Outline palms in 3 tip forest green. Let set.
3. Fill in trunk with 4 tip medium brown.
4. Fill in palms with 4 or 5 tip bright green. Let set.

Details:

5. Pipe three dots with 3 tip dark brown for coconuts.

Shell

(See templates on page 92.)

You'll need:

3 tip black

4 tip white

Note: You may substitute any bright color for the outline color.

1. Outline design with 3 tip black. Let set.
2. Fill in with 4 tip white.

Down on the Farm

Pig
(See templates on page 93.)

You'll need:
3 and 2 tip black
5 tip light pink
2 tip hot pink

1. Outline design with 3 tip black. Let set.
2. Fill in with 5 tip light pink. Let set.

Details:
3. Pipe an eye and a mouth with 2 tip black.
4. Pipe curlicue with 2 tip hot pink.

Horse
(See templates on page 93.)

You'll need:
3 and 2 tip black
5 tip medium brown
3 tip dark brown
3 and 2 tip light brown
2 tip white

1. Outline design in 3 tip black. Let set
2. Fill in horse with 5 tip medium brown. Let set.
3. Fill in hooves with 3 tip dark brown.
4. Fill in tail with 3 tip light brown.

Details:
5. Pipe eye and mouth with 2 tip black.
6. Pipe stripe on muzzle with 2 tip white.
7. Pipe mane with 2 tip light brown.

Hey There, Sport!

Football

(See templates on page 94.)

You'll need:
3 tip black
5 tip medium brown
4 tip white

1. Outline design with 3 tip black. Let set
2. Fill in football with 5 tip brown.
3. Fill in stripes and laces with 4 tip white.

Baseball

(See templates on page 94.)

You'll need:
3 tip black
5 tip white
2 tip red

1. Outline design with 3 tip black. Let set.
2. Fill in with 5 tip white. Let set.

Details:
3. Pipe stitching with 2 tip red.

Basketball

(See templates on page 94.)

You'll need:
3 and 2 tip black
4 tip orange

1. Outline circle with 3 tip black. Let set.
2. Fill in with 4 tip orange. Let set.

Details:
3. Pipe basketball lines with 2 tip black.

Sassy Style

Little Black Dress
(See templates on page 95.)

You'll need:
3 and 4 tip black
3 and 2 tip hot pink
2 tip slime green

1. Outline design with 3 tip black. Let set.
2. Fill in dress with 4 tip black. Let set.
3. Fill in belt with 3 tip hot pink.

Details:
4. Pipe a dot with 2 tip slime green for flower center.
5. Pipe five dots around the green with 2 tip hot pink to complete flower.

Shoe
(See templates on page 95.)

You'll need:
3 and 4 tip black
3 and 2 tip slime green
2 tip hot pink

1. Outline design with 3 tip black. Let set.
2. Fill in shoe with 4 tip black. Let set.
3. Fill in sole with 3 tip slime green.

Details:
5. Pipe dot on strap with 2 tip slime green.
6. Pipe five dots around green dot with 2 tip hot pink.

Certificate of Birth

This hereby certifies that:

Cutie Pie

was born on:

The Sunniest Day of the Year

Weight: 2 teddy bears heavy

Length: 4 rattles long

Awww . . . Baby

Footprint
(See templates on page 96.)

You'll need:
4 (or 5) tip baby blue, light pink, or a gender-neutral pastel

1. Outline foot (not including toes) with 4 tip. Let set.
2. Fill in with 4 or 5 tip.
3. With 4 tip, make five dots for toes, starting with the big toe and getting progressively smaller.

Carriage
(See templates on page 96.)

You'll need:
3 tip medium purple
4 tip white
5 tip lavender
5 tip light slime green

Note: You can substitute any pastel colors.

1. Outline design with 3 tip medium purple. Let set.
2. Fill in carriage with 4 tip white.
3. Fill in blanket and wheels with 5 tip lavender.
4. Fill in hood and center of wheels with 5 tip light slime green.

Flitters and Critters

Bee

(See templates on page 97.)

You'll need:
3 tip black
4 tip white
4 tip butter yellow

1. Outline bee with 3 tip black. Let set.
2. Fill in head and stripes with 3 tip black.
3. Fill in wings with 4 tip white.
4. Fill in body with 4 tip butter yellow.

Worm

(See templates on page 97.)

You'll need:
3 tip bright green
4 tip slime green
3 tip white
2 tip black
4 tip light slime green

1. Outline design with 3 tip bright green.
   Let set.
2. Fill in with 4 tip slime green. Let set.

Details:
3. Pipe two white eyes with 3 tip. Let set.
4. Pipe two black eyes in white and smiley
   face with 2 tip black.
5. Pipe highlights with 4 tip light slime green.

Butterfly

(See templates on page 97.)

You'll need:
3 tip burnt orange
3 tip bright green
3 tip hot pink
4 tip orange
4 tip slime green
4 tip medium pink

1. Outline body with 3 tip burnt orange.
   Let set.
2. Outline top half of wings and lower inner-
   wing design with 3 tip bright green. Let set.
3. Outline lower half of wings and upper inner-
   wing design with 3 tip hot pink. Let set.
4. Fill in body with 4 tip orange.
5. Fill in upper wings and lower inner-wing
   design with 4 tip slime green.
6. Fill in lower wings and upper inner-wing
   design with 4 tip medium pink.

Pretty Things That Grow

Sunflower

(See templates on page 98.)

You'll need:
5 tip medium brown
3 tip gold
4 tip butter yellow
3 tip baby yellow
4 tip baby blue

1. With 5 tip brown, outline sunflower center. Let set.
2. With 3 tip gold, outline petals. Let set.
3. Fill in sunflower center with 5 tip brown. Let set.
4. Fill in petals with 4 tip butter yellow.

Details:

5. With 3 tip baby yellow, draw swirl on top of sunflower center.
6. With 4 tip baby blue, squeeze small petals in between yellow petals.

Daisy

(See templates on page 98.)

You'll need:
3 tip gold
3 tip hot pink
4 tip butter yellow
5 tip medium pink

Note: Any bright color and a lighter version of the same color to fill in can be substituted for the pink.

1. Outline center with 3 tip gold. Let set.
2. Outline petals with 3 tip hot pink. Let set.
3. Fill in center with 4 tip butter yellow.
4. Fill in petals with 5 tip medium pink.

Cocktail Hour

Martini

(See templates on page 99.)

You'll need:
3 tip black
3 tip forest green
3 tip white
4 tip bright green
3 tip red
4 tip gray

Note: You can make a cosmopolitan with the same outline. Just omit the olive, and fill in the drink with a medium pink and a light pink highlight. Keep the glass background white.

1. Outline design with 3 tip black. Let set.
2. Outline olive with 3 tip forest green. Let set.
3. Fill in martini and glass background with 3 tip white.
4. Fill in olive with 4 tip bright green.

Details:
5. Pipe dot in olive with 3 tip red.
6. Pipe highlight with 4 tip gray.

Margarita

(See templates on page 99.)

You'll need:
3 tip black
3 tip slime green
3 tip bright green
4 tip light slime green
3 and 2 tip white

1. Outline glass with 3 tip black. Let set.
2. Outline liquid with 3 tip slime green. Let set.
3. Outline lime slice with 3 tip bright green. Let set.
4. Fill in drink with 4 tip light slime green.
5. Fill in lime slice with 3 tip slime green. Let set.
6. Fill in glass background with 3 tip white.

Details:
7. Pipe lime sections with 2 tip white.

Here Comes the Bride (and Groom)

Note: Let the outline and background set a good fifteen minutes or so for the wedding cookies, because you are filling and making details with the same color.

Wedding Dress
(See templates on page 100.)

You'll need:
3, 5, and 2 tip white

1. Outline design in 3 tip white. Let set.
2. Fill in with 5 tip white. Let set.

Details:
3. Pipe dots and swirls with 2 tip white.

Tuxedo
(See templates on pages 100–101.)

You'll need:
3, 4, and 2 tip black
3 tip white
2 tip butter yellow
2 tip baby blue

1. Outline design with 3 tip black.
2. Fill in between lapels with 3 tip white. Let set.
3. Fill in tuxedo with 4 tip black. Let set.

Details:
4. Pipe bow tie and buttons with 2 tip black.
5. Pipe dot on lapel with 2 tip butter yellow.
6. Pipe five dots around yellow with 2 tip baby blue for flower.

Wedding Cake
(See templates on page 101.)

You'll need:
3 and 5 tip white
2 tip assortment of pastels (baby yellow, light slime green, baby blue, light pink and /or lavender) or you can use 2 tip white

1. Pipe outline with 3 tip white. Let set.
2. Fill in with 5 tip white. Let set.

Details:
3. With 2 tip pastels or with all white, pipe dots for flowers (one dot in center with five dots surrounding).
4. With 2 tip white, pipe swirls.

For Your Honey

Heart

(See templates on page 102.)

You'll need:
3 tip burgundy
5 tip red
2 tip white and/or pink

1. Outline heart with 3 tip burgundy. Let set.
2. Fill in heart with 5 tip red. Let set.

Details:
3. With 2 tip white and/or pink, pipe designs (stripes, dots, checkered pattern, or swirls).

Trick or Treat

Cauldron
(See templates on page 102.)

You'll need:
3 and 5 tip black
3 tip bright green
4 tip slime green
2 tip white

1. Outline cauldron with 3 tip black. Let set.
2. Outline cauldron concoction and bubbles with 3 tip bright green. Let set.
3. Fill in cauldron (using caution around bubble outlines) with 5 tip black.
4. Fill in concoction and bubbles with 4 tip slime green. Let set.

Details:
5. Pipe highlights in concoction and bubbles with 2 tip white.

Ghost
(See templates on page 102.)

You'll need:
3, 4, and 2 tip white
2 tip black

1. Outline design with 3 tip white. Let set.
2. Fill in with 4 tip white. Let set.

Details:
3. Pipe eyes and a screaming mouth with 2 tip black.
4. Pipe swirls and dots with 2 tip white.

Free Falling

Autumn Leaf

(See templates on page 103.)

You'll need:

4 tip dark brown

4 tip orange

4 tip gold

4 tip butter yellow

Note: Any mixture of fall colors works, such as burgundy, orange, and all shades of yellow, but keep the veins dark brown.

1. Pipe *only* leaf stem and veins with 4 tip dark brown. Do *not* pipe outline of the cookie shape. Let set.
2. Pipe around leaf stem and veins with 4 tip orange.
3. Pipe around orange with 4 tip gold to fill most of the cookie, leaving tips of leaves bare.
4. Pipe tips of leaves with 4 tip butter yellow.

Happy Hanukkah

Dreidel
(See templates on page 104.)

You'll need:
3 and 2 tip royal blue
4 tip white

1. Outline design with 3 tip royal blue. Let set.
2. Fill in with 4 tip white. Let set.

Details:
3. Pipe Hebrew letters with 2 tip royal blue.

Six-Pointed Star
(See templates on page 104.)

You'll need:
3 and 4 tip royal blue
4 tip bright blue
4 tip white

1. Outline design with 3 tip royal blue. Let set.
2. Fill in one "triangle" with 4 tip royal blue.
3. Fill in other "triangle" with 4 tip bright blue, working around the royal blue "triangle."
4. Fill in background with 4 tip white.

Winter Wonderland

Snowflake

(See templates on page 105.)

You'll need:
4 tip baby blue (or mint green)
2 tip white

Note: You can reverse the colors, so the background is white and the snowflake design is in color.

1. Outline cookie with 4 tip baby blue.
2. Fill in with 4 tip baby blue. Let set.

Details:
3. Pipe snowflake design with 2 tip white.

Snowman

(See templates on page 105.)

You'll need:
3, 4, and 2 tip black
4 tip white
3 tip orange
4 tip bright green
2 and 3 tip slime green
2 tip medium brown

1. Outline hat and scarf with 3 tip black.
   Let set.
2. Outline snowman head and body with 4 tip white. Let set.
3. Fill in snowman head and body with 4 tip white. Let set.
4. Fill in hat with 4 tip black.
5. Fill in band on hat and scarf with 4 tip bright green. Let set.

Details:
6. Pipe triangle for carrot nose with 3 tip orange. (Squeeze bag at center of face and pull to the left, letting the piping naturally fall into a triangle.)
7. Pipe smiley face with 2 tip black.
8. Pipe fringe and lines on scarf with 2 tip slime green.
9. Pipe buttons with 3 tip slime green.
10. Pipe tree branch arms with 2 tip medium brown.

Jingle Bells

Stocking

(See templates on page 106.)

You'll need:
3 tip black
4 tip white
4 tip red
4 tip slime green
4 tip bright green

1. Outline design with 3 tip black. Let set.
2. Fill in cuff with 4 tip white.
3. Fill in alternating stripes with 4 tip red.
4. Fill in alternating stripes with 4 tip slime green.
5. Fill in toe and heel with 4 tip bright green.

Candy Cane

(See templates on page 106.)

You'll need:
3 tip burgundy
4 tip white
4 tip red
2 tip bright green

1. Outline design with 3 tip burgundy. Let set.
2. Fill in alternating stripes with 4 tip white. Let set.
3. Fill in alternating stripes with 4 tip red.

Details:
4. Pipe stripes on white with 2 tip bright green.

One Big Happy Family

Note: If using gingerbread dough, there is no need to fill in the cookie with light brown. Just keep the background undecorated, but outline the body and fill in the clothing as instructed.

Gingerbread Man
(See templates on page 107.)

You'll need:
3 tip forest green
3 tip medium brown
3 tip burgundy
5 tip light brown (optional, see note)
4 tip red
4 tip bright green
2 tip black
2 tip white

1. Outline pants and suspenders with 3 tip forest green. Let set.
2. Outline body (around pants and suspenders) with 3 tip medium brown. Let set.
3. Outline tie with 3 tip burgundy. Let set.
4. Fill in body with 5 tip light brown. Let set. (Optional, see note.)
5. Fill in tie with 4 tip red.
6. Fill in pants and suspenders with 4 tip bright green.

Details:
7. Pipe big dot for nose with 4 tip red.
8. Pipe smiley face with 2 tip black.
9. Pipe squiggles and buttons with 2 tip white.

Gingerbread Woman
(See templates on page 108.)

You'll need:
3 tip forest green
3 tip medium brown
5 tip light brown (optional, see note)
4 tip bright green
4 tip white
4 and 2 tip red
2 tip black

1. Outline dress and apron with 3 tip forest green. Let set.
2. Outline body (around dress) with 3 tip medium brown. Let set.
3. Fill in body with 5 tip light brown. Let set. (Optional, see note.)
5. Fill in dress with 4 tip bright green. Let set.
6. Fill in apron and strap with 4 tip white. Let set.

Details:
7. Pipe big dot for nose with 4 tip red.
8. Pipe smiley face with 2 tip black.
9. Pipe bow, buttons, apron bow, and edge of apron with 2 tip red.

Practice Shapes

A a B b C c

R r S s T t U u

0 1 2 3 4 5

Happy
Birthday

Know Your ABCs

Letter
(A)

(B)

Space Invaders

Spaceship
(A)

(B)

(C)

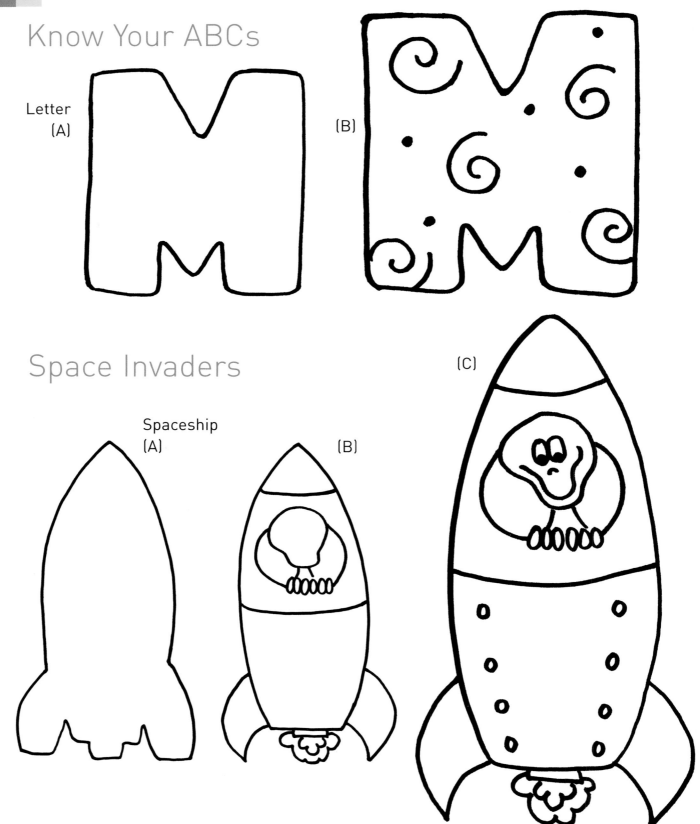

Under the Sea

Fish
(A)

(B)

(C)

Octopus
(A)

(B)

(C)

A Day at the Beach

Palm Tree
(A)

(B)

(B)

Shell (A)

Down on the Farm

Pig (A)

(B)

(C)

Horse (A)

(C)

(B)

Hey There, Sport

Football (A)   (B)

Baseball &
Basketball (A)

(B)

(B)

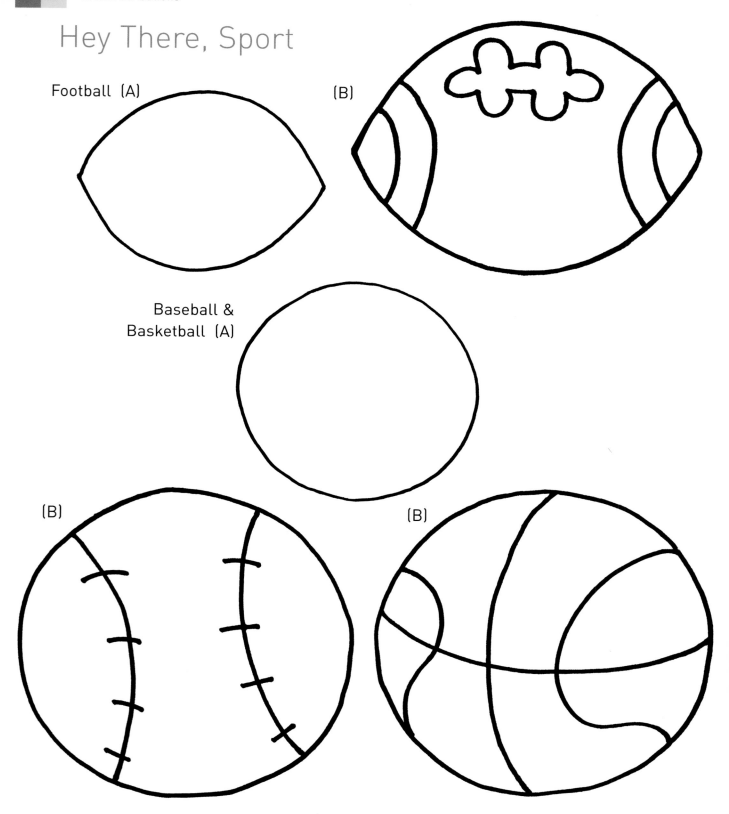

Sassy Style

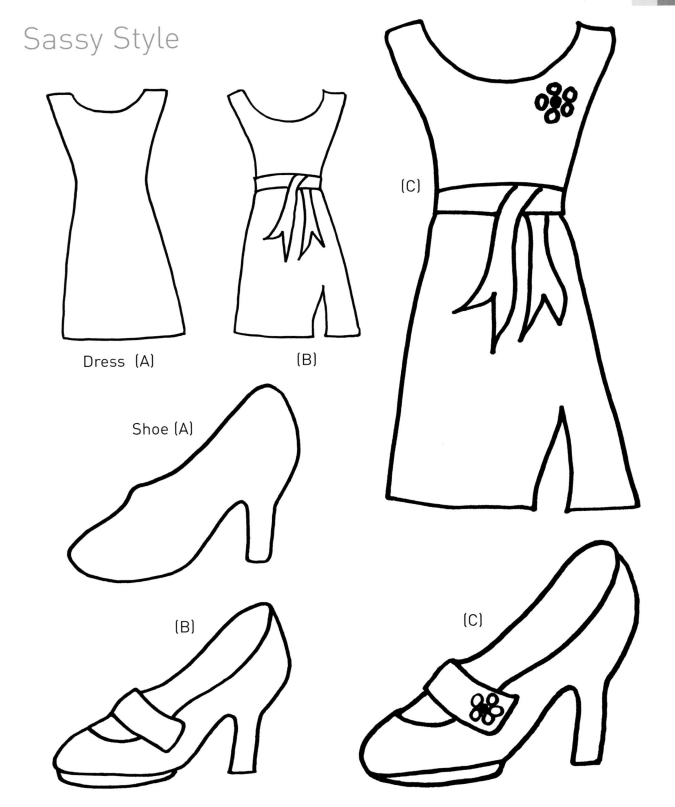

Dress (A)

(B)

(C)

Shoe (A)

(B)

(C)

Awww...Baby

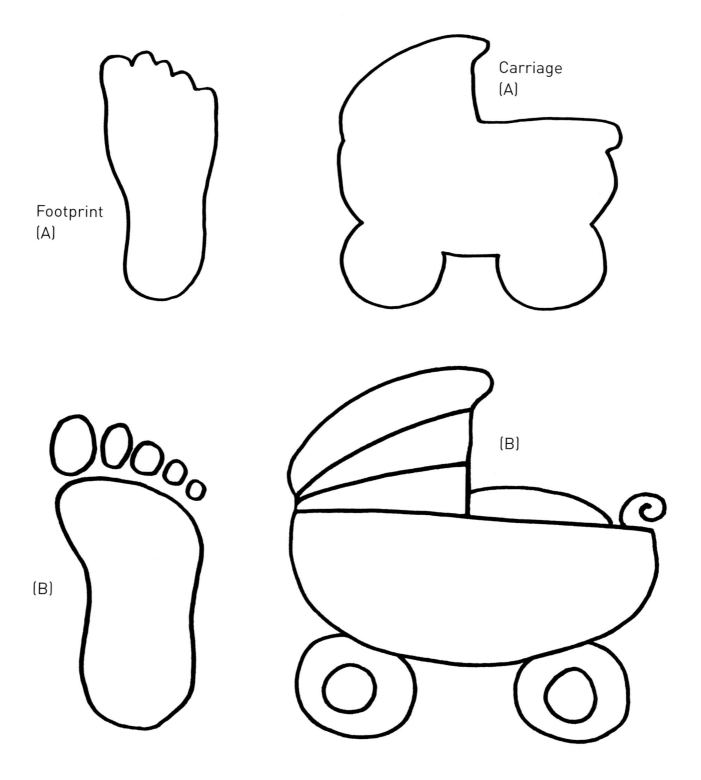

Footprint
(A)

Carriage
(A)

(B)

(B)

Flitters and Critters

Bee (A)

(B)

Worm (A)

(B)

Butterfly (A)

(B)

Pretty Things That Grow

Sunflower (A)

(B)

(C)

Daisy (A)

(B)

Cocktail Hour

Martini (A)

(B)

(C)

Margarita (A)

(B)

(C)

Here Comes the Bride (and Groom)

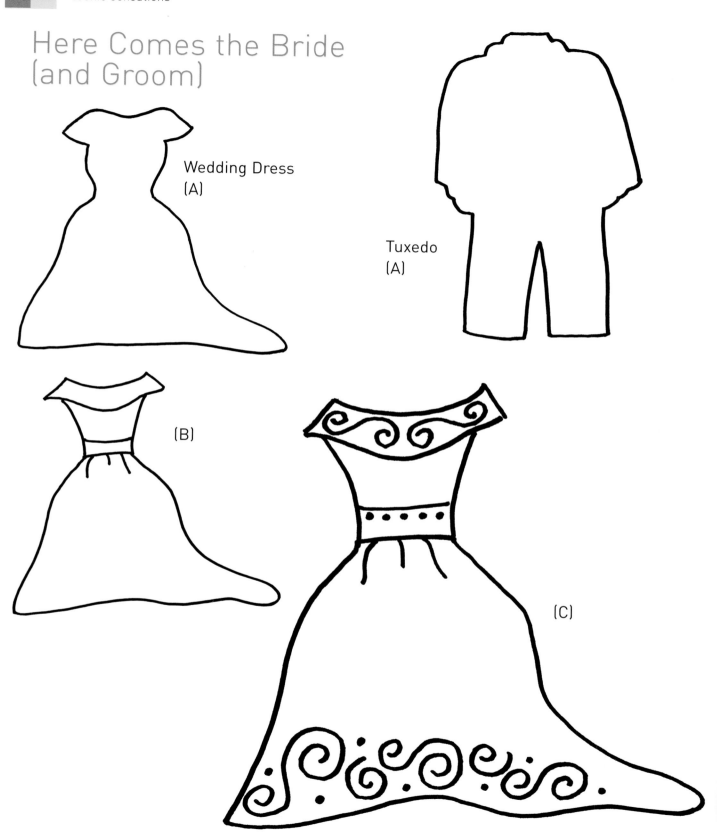

Wedding Dress (A)

Tuxedo (A)

(B)

(C)

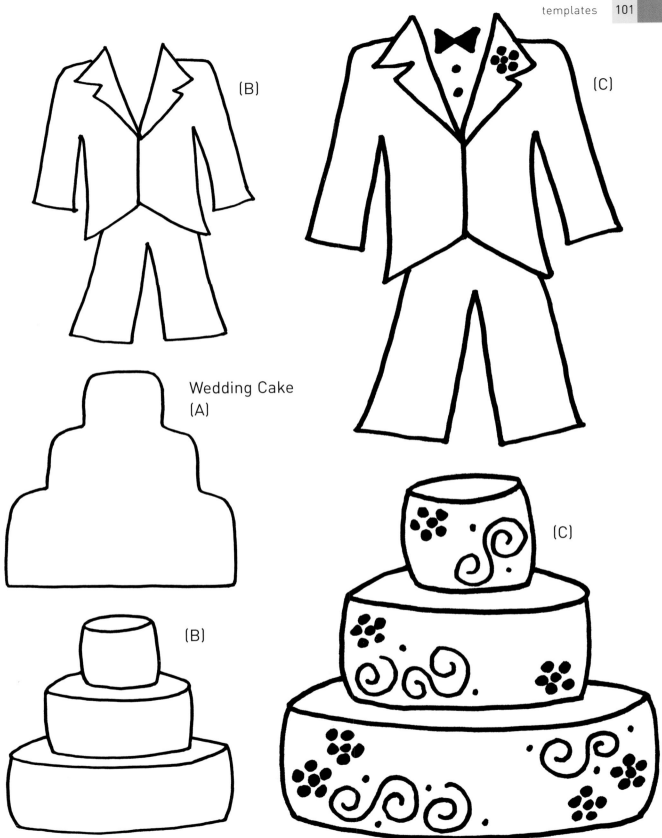

(B)

(C)

Wedding Cake
(A)

(B)

(C)

For Your Honey

Heart
(A)

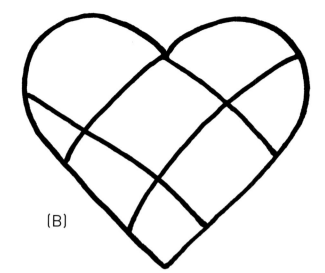

(B)

Trick or Treat

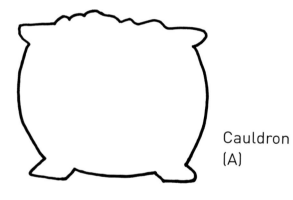

Cauldron
(A)

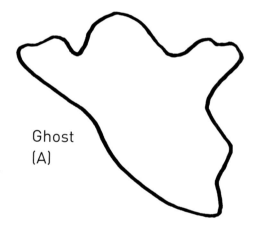

Ghost
(A)

(B)

(B)

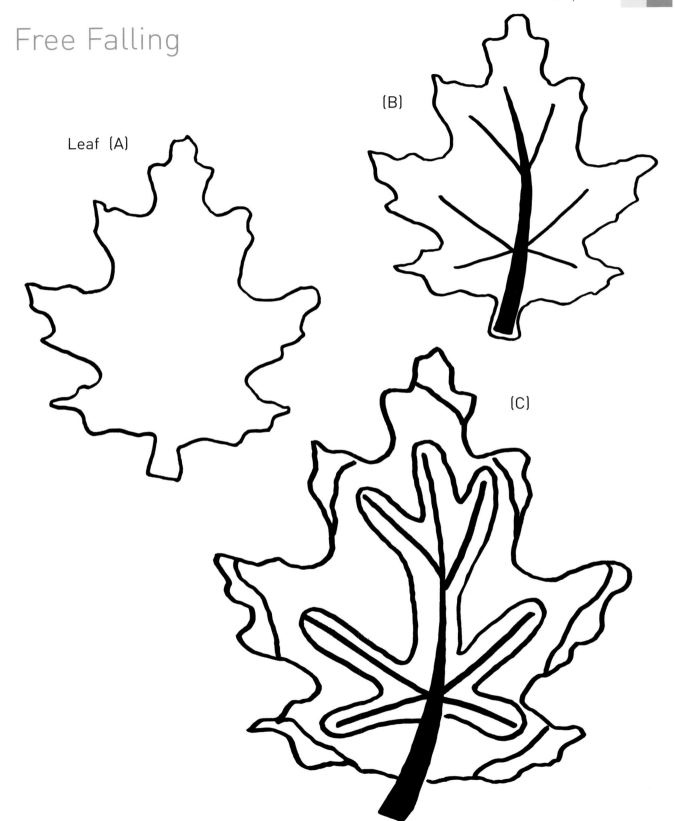

Free Falling

Leaf (A)

(B)

(C)

Happy Hanukkah

Dreidel
(A)

(B)

(C)

Six-Pointed Star
(A)

(B)

Winter Wonderland

Snowflake (A)

(B)

Snowman (A)

(B)

(C)

Jingle Bells

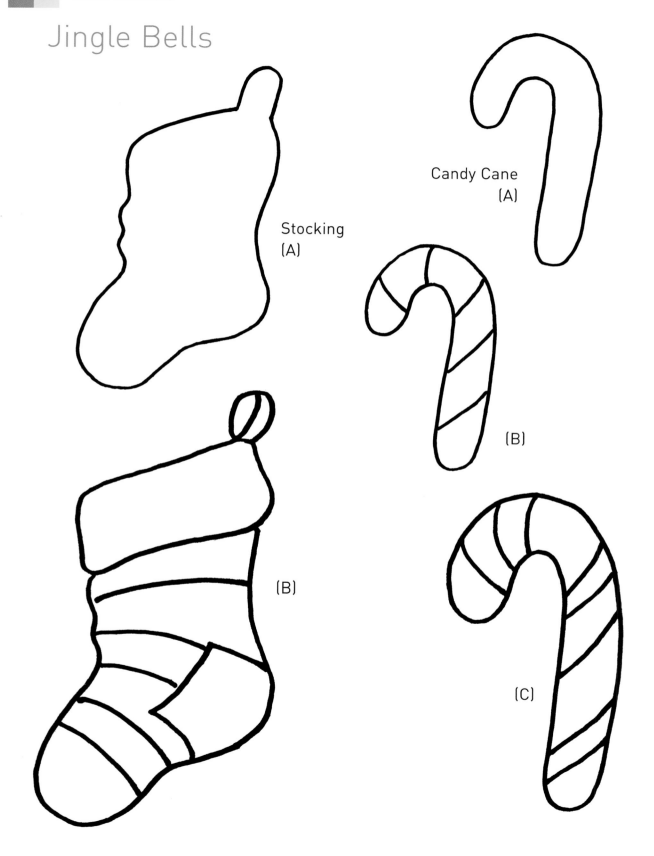

Candy Cane
(A)

Stocking
(A)

(B)

(B)

(C)

One Big Happy Family

Gingerbread Man
(A)

(B)

(C)

Gingerbread Woman
(A)

(B)

(C)

8

Wrapping It Up:
Cookie Gifts

Chances are, many of the decorated cookies you make will be gifts or for others. All that hard work just to sit and eat them yourself? Unlikely. And chances are, you've put much thought into exactly what you want to say with your decorated cookies by choosing particular shapes, designs, and colors. The creativity doesn't end with the cookies. Careful presentation means not only pleasing the eye—but also doing your best to avoid smushing all your precious work. Here you'll find ideas for using your cookies and the best ways to package them.

Wrapping your Cookies

Inexpensive, clear, cellophane favor bags are available at most craft and party stores. After the frosting dries to the touch—ideally, let it dry overnight—gently place a cookie in a cellophane favor bag and tie closed with coordinating ribbon. Be especially careful if you use Buttercream Frosting, as it will still be slightly soft, even if dried overnight. You may want to arrange the cookies on a platter for use at a party for guests to nibble on (and admire and highly praise). If you are shipping cookies, however, you should definitely use Royal Icing, because this type of frosting dries harder.

If you are boxing cookies or putting them in tins, gently lay them in place and don't jostle the box as heartily as you might with undecorated cookies. Even if the icing has dried overnight, little bits and pieces might fall off. And—this is very important—if you are using tissue paper to line the box or tin, include a layer of clear cellophane or wax paper between the tissue and the cookies. Even if the cookie feels dry, grease will gradually soak into tissue paper, making for an unappetizing presentation when the box is opened.

To wrap a platter filled with cookies to give as a gift, rip a large piece off a roll of clear cellophane. Center the plate on top of the cellophane, gather the edges of the cellophane at the top, and tie tightly with a decorative ribbon.

Say It with Cookies

At the store, we make baskets of cookies with specific themes—any theme, really, you can possibly imagine or invent. Birthdays, weddings, holidays of every type, bar and bat mitzvahs, retirement parties, anniversaries, corporate gifts,

thank-yous, apologies, graduations, welcomes to the neighborhood, bon voyages, get wells, congratulations, new babies, well wishes, and on and on. Our customers use the cookies in many different ways, and we offer many gift-giving ideas, some of which are included here.

Accents for gifts. Tie a wrapped cookie to a package or add to a gift basket. Possibilities include a wedding dress cookie for a bridal shower gift; a snowman or snowflake cookie added to a basket with mugs, hot cocoa, and marshmallows; or a candle cookie attached to a birthday gift.

Substitute gifts. That perfect sweater didn't arrive in time for the birthday? The gift is a day at the spa or something intangible? Or a new bright red sports car that doesn't fit in a box? Give a sweater cookie with a tag that says "Coming Soon," cookies in the shape of a hair dryer and a bottle of nail polish with the spa gift certificate, or a cookie with a bright red car design. Want to treat someone to a movie? Give them a cookie ticket.

Additions to wedding guests' welcome bags. You can make hearts, a bride and groom, or cookies related to the host city, such as the White House, the Space Needle, a Georgia peach, a cactus or cowboy boot for a Southwest wedding, an evergreen for a Northern wedding. At my Las Vegas wedding, each guest had an Elvis, slot machine, cards, or dice.

Place cards that double as favors. (First you need to master writing, of course.) Write your guests' names on pumpkins or turkeys and put a cookie on each plate at the Thanksgiving table. Or stockings for Christmas dinner. Or Easter eggs for Easter dinner. Or dreidels for Hanukkah dinner. Or hearts for a rehearsal dinner. You get the idea.

Dessert at a theme party. Cosmopolitan and martini cookies will make a hit at a cocktail party. Make football and helmet cookies with your team's colors for a

Super Bowl party. At your Fourth of July picnic, put out a plate of flags, stars, and firecracker cookies.

Take-home favors at any party. The possibilities are endless: footprints for a baby shower, hearts or bridal gowns and bridesmaid dresses at a wedding shower, lingerie at a bachelorette party, playing cards for a poker party, champagne glasses for New Year's Eve, shamrocks for St. Patty's Day, dinosaurs or princesses for your child's birthday party, and so on.

Thank-you gifts. Make dog or cat cookies for the pet-sitter, chalkboard and school bus cookies for your child's teacher, letter cookies for the mail carrier, newspaper cookies for the delivery boy or girl, or flower cookies for a supportive friend.

Cake toppers to decorate a finished cake. Make button or ducky cookies

to adorn a cake at a baby shower, or number cookies for a birthday cake. Use smaller cookies and roll them thin, no more than one-eighth of an inch. The lighter, the better—otherwise the cookies will weigh down the cake.

Host or hostess gifts. Purchase a nice plate or platter and fill with decorated cookies such as small hearts for an engagement party. Or bring hot dog, hamburger, or watermelon cookies to a barbecue. Wrap with cellophane as instructed above.

Final Words

I started at Bundles of Cookies in 1998 on a lark, thinking it a temporary job. Almost a decade later, I can truly say that cookies have changed my life. Or at least formed an unusually large part of it! Turning sugar, flour, butter, and food color into beautiful creations is a marvelous feat. But how the cookies are used is what makes cookie making and decorating so fascinating. Daily and yearly, our customers come up with design ideas to put on cookies based on what they want to say to the recipients of these tasty treats. They thoughtfully express happiness, well wishes, sympathies, apologies, and love to others through our cookies. Customers are thrilled when we can put their inside jokes, their beloved pets, their favorite characters, and even their own drawings on cookies. They often are shocked when we say, "Sure, of course we can do that!" And we play the role of artful mediator between gift givers and recipients.

You can take our knowledge into your own kitchen and truly personalize your cookies. Use them as conversation at every turn of life, but be warned: This is a transient art. While I hear stories of customers claiming to keep our cookies for years in their china cabinet, they are perishable goods designed and destined to be consumed. Consumed, but not forgotten. And that is part of the joy.

Bibliography

Chaucer, Geoffrey. "The Tale of Sir Thopas." *The Canterbury Tales.* From the Hengwrt Manuscript. Edited by N. F. Blake. London: Edward Arnold Publishers Ltd., 1980.

Cowper, William. "Table Talk." *The Complete Poetical Works of William Cowper. With Life, and Critical Notice of His Writings.* Boston, Mass.: Gould and Lincoln. www.ccel.org/c/cowper/works/cowperwk.rtf

Dawson, Thomas. *The Good Huswifes Jewell.* 1596. East Sussex, England: Southover Press, 1996.

Franklin, Linda Campbell. *300 Years of Kitchen Collectibles.* 5th ed. Iola, Wisc.: Krause Publications, 2003.

Greaser, Arlene and Paul H. *Cookie Cutters and Molds.* Allentown, Penn.: Arlene and Paul H. Greaser, 1969.

Grimm, Jacob and Wilhelm. "Hansel and Gretel." 1812. Edited by Maria Tatar. *The Annotated Classic Fairy Tales.* New York: W. W. Norton & Co., 2002.

Haber, Barbara. *From Hardtack to Home Fries: An Uncommon History of American Cooks and Meals.* New York: The Free Press, 2002.

Hudgins, Sharon. "Edible Art: Springerle Cookies." *Gastronomica: The Journal of Food and Culture* 4, no. 4 (2004): 66–71.

Martha Washington's Booke of Cookery and Booke of Sweetmeats. Transcribed by Karen Hess. New York: Columbia University Press, 1981.

Ross, Alice. "A Gingerbread Tradition." *Journal of Antiques and Collectibles.* December 2000. www.journalofantiques.com/hearthdec.htm

Shakespeare, William. *Love's Labour's Lost.* The Kittredge Shakespeare. Edited by George Lyman Kittredge. Waltham, Mass.: Glaisdell Publishing Co., 1968.

Simmons, Amelia. *The First American Cookbook: A Facsimile of "American Cookery," 1796.* Mineola, N.Y.: Dover Publications, 1981.

Stellingwerf, Steven. *The Gingerbread Book.* New York: Rizzoli International Publications, 1991.

Stephens, David. *The Gingerbread Man and Tales You'll Enjoy.* Atlanta, Georgia: Center for Puppetry Arts, 2002. www.puppet.org/pdf/gingerstgd.pdf

Stradley, Linda. "History of Cookies." *I'll Have What They're Having—Legendary Local Cuisine.* Falcon, 2002. http://whatscookingamerica.net/History/CookieHistory.htm

Stavely, Keith and Kathleen Fitzgerald. *America's Founding Food: The Story of New England Cooking.* Chapel Hill, N.C.: The University of North Carolina Press, 2004.

Wetherill, Phyllis Steiss. *An Encyclopedia of Cookie Shaping.* Washington, D.C.: Phyllis Steiss Wetherill, 1981.

Wilson, Mary Tolford. Essay, "The First American Cookbook." *The First American Cookbook: A Facsimile of "American Cookery," 1796.* Mineola, New York: Dover Publications, 1981, pp. vii–xxiv.

Wordsworth, Dorothy. *The Grasmere Journals.* Edited by Pamela Woof. Oxford: Oxford University Press, 1991.

MEAGHAN MOUNTFORD is head decorator of Bundles of Cookies in Bethesda, Maryland. Her cookies have been featured on the *Today* show and in the *New York Times*, and her store was named "Best of Washington" by the *Washingtonian*. Among her longtime clients are top corporations, media networks, professional sports teams, and both Washington and Hollywood celebrities.